In Response to Obedience

HOW GOD USED LOVE, PRAYER,
FAITH, AND HOPE TO BUILD A MINISTRY
WITH ONE WOMAN'S RESPONSE.

PAULA FRENCH
WITH REOVA MEREDITH

WESTBOW
PRESS®
A DIVISION OF THOMAS NELSON
& ZONDERVAN

WestBow Press books may be ordered through booksellers or by contacting:

WestBow Press
A Division of Thomas Nelson & Zondervan
1663 Liberty Drive
Bloomington, IN 47403
www.westbowpress.com
844-714-3454

ISBN: 979-8-3850-3824-4 (sc)
ISBN: 979-8-3850-3823-7 (e)

Library of Congress Control Number: 2024924457

Print information available on the last page.

WestBow Press rev. date: 12/18/2024

Contents

Introduction

The Center for Women's Ministry is non-profit, peer-counseling ministry for women ages 13 and above that offers free counseling, support groups, Bible studies, and prayer groups to foster spiritual and emotional healing. All of the volunteers are trained in a 14-week educational program that covers counseling techniques, issues, policies, and procedures. In addition to the Basic 14-week training, ongoing training is required by all those who counsel clients.

Today, at this writing, The Center for Women's Ministry has over 35 Centers in 7 states and 6 international countries and is growing daily. The ministry motto, "We've been where you are" resonates with women in need of counsel or direction, or a listening ear, since many of the volunteers were once clients of the same ministry. The ministry has an incredible, dedicated staff, Board of Directors, and countless volunteers who all prayerfully serve to bring hope to the hurting. The ministry was born when one woman wholly believed that God would do mighty things in response to her obedience to Him.

Chapter One

THE MEETING

It was the mid-nineties, and my family had recently moved to Indianapolis. The phone rang and on the other end was my long-time friend, Konda. Our kids had grown up going to church camps together and most often we went with them, acting more like campers than counselors. Outside of that one week we spent together each summer, Konda lived her life and I lived mine, separated by half a state. But we were both fiercely believing moms and active members of the same denomination, and that bonded us more than 7am inspections, magic marker mustaches, and silly skits.

"Hey, remember my friend, Reova Meredith at church?" Konda began the conversation. "I think I told you about her. She's the one that has started a counseling ministry here in Bloomington. Well, other counties are wanting to start centers, and it's getting to be a lot for her to travel and train volunteers herself. She's thinking she needs a training manual so she can train a few women, and they can use the manual to train others. I told her you were a writer getting your Master's degree in Counseling and we wondered if you might like to help?"

A few weeks later on a Saturday afternoon at Schapiro's Deli on 86th Street, I met Konda, and for the first time, Reova. We had a lovely lunch discussion, and I walked away with a box of notes and a brain full of ideas of what the first Training Manual for the Center for Women's Ministries would entail. I remember the first manual only needed minimal techniques, like listening skills, confidentiality, and building client rapport. I also remember it was only about ½ inch thick and didn't even need a Table of Contents. But what I remember more than all of that was meeting Reova Meredith.

Her bigger-than-life presence and Godly reputation got there way ahead of her. As it often happens, we are drawn to women who have navigated raising children and lived to tell about it. The fact that she had also wrestled with God and was now following His unique plan for her life made her irresistible. She made me want to be a part of it to see what would happen!

Reova was warm and obviously intelligent but had this sense of humor and easy laugh. Beneath all of that, however, was a serious, head-down, shoulders-to-the-wind follower of Christ. And following Him she was—though she had little idea where He was leading her.

I wouldn't hear her entire story until much later, but in that first meeting, I heard and saw enough to respect her, trust her, and love her immediately. This is her story. She would say that it is God's story. And while that is true, it is the story of how God taught a believing schoolteacher that if she would obey Him in everything He asked, He would do amazing things. And she did. And He has!

Throughout my years with the Center For Women's Ministries, I have been a part of many of the Leadership Intensive Trainings, held every other year at different Indiana campgrounds. While the women and late-night sharing sessions may have differed each year, one highlight remained the same – Reova's five famous devotions. Each day began at 7 a.m. with Reova sharing the five requirements for a vibrant and productive relationship with Christ. Without these five requirements working together, Love, Prayer, Obedience, Faith, and Hope, the Christian journey is incomplete and lacks fruitfulness. These devotions are scattered here amidst her story where each played its rightful part, divinely planted by the One who was growing the Center For Women's Ministries one surrendered volunteer at a time. And it all began with Reova!

Chapter Two

REOVA SHARES HER BEGINNING

I grew up in a pastor's home, the oldest of seven children, six girls and one boy. Because my Dad was a pastor, church was the biggest part of our lives, and I became a Christian when I was very young child. I lived a very consistent Christian life throughout my life there in south central Indiana, where we lived a normal, conservative life.

After college, while teaching, I met Doug, who had just returned from Korea as a U.S. Marine. He had enrolled as a student at the Bible College, and after a year we were married and headed off to Bloomington for his new job at Indiana University. We stayed there for over 30 years where I taught school while we raised our three sons.

I had always hoped to marry a minister, like my Mom did, but that did not happen. Instead, I found myself struggling being married to someone who grew up in the child protection system and spent his young adult years dealing with active military combat.

At the time, of course, I never realized the effects either one of those experiences could have on a person, much less both of them, but I lived the resulting difficulties daily as I tried to navigate marriage, motherhood, and myself.

When I got it to my mid-40's, the Lord began to deal with me about a closer, more intimate walk with Him. I describe it as a large circle with Christ in the middle. If we have not yet found Jesus as our personal Savior, we are outside of that circle. After we receive Him as our Savior, we move into the inside of that circle. We can choose to live anywhere we want within that circle. Once inside, we can dabble around the edges, or we can move closer to the center where Christ is. But if we decide to do that, there will be some requirements made of us that Christ would not require of us if we continued to dabble around the edges of it.

So, in my mid-40s, in my search for a more intimate walk with the Lord, I told Him I wanted to live as close to Him as I could– right in the center. I wanted to be able to crawl up on His lap and hear Him say "I'm pleased with what you're doing, and I love you." Out of that quest grew something that I never had any idea would change my life like it did.

Love

"If our girls really knew how much God loves them, healing would come!"

-Reova Meredith

It All Began With LOVE
The Most Powerful Force in Life

God's Love for us... leads to... **Our love for God...** leads to...**Our love for others**

What is Love? Where did it come from? Why is it in our world? Is it necessary for survival? What if we don't have it?

Webster defines love as both a noun and a verb. As a noun, love is defined as a strong affection, warm attachment, or an attraction to someone or something. It's a feeling. As a verb, love is defined as holding someone or something dear, cherishing and finding pleasure in that person or object. There are typically accompanying actions required to prove you are holding the person or object dear, or to prove you are cherishing or finding pleasure in them.

Where love comes from and why it is in our world is both tricky and simple. If love is in our world, it had to be put here by our creator, God. The Bible doesn't say "On the third day God created love." But it does tell us about all the ways God showed love (the verb) to us by all the amazing and necessary things He created for us. And He obviously created within us a capacity to love, as was shown many times throughout the Bible and is evident in our own lives. The Bible also tells us that God created man "in His own image" (Genesis 1:27), so if we have a capacity to love, we can assume God also has the capacity to love.

In fact, the Bible is clear that God is the source and initiator of love. I John 4:7-10, and 19, tells us these things; *Dear friends... love comes from God. Whoever does not love does not know God, because God is love.... This is love: not that we loved God, but that he loved us and sent his Son as an atoning sacrifice for our sins.... God is love... We love because he first loved us.* It is impossible for us to love without God. God's very nature is love, and we love only because He first loved us. Many people question God's love because of all the terrible things in the world He could prevent. That is a reasonable, human viewpoint when we don't fully understand or acknowledge His Sovereignty or His original perfect plan for His creation, which He will someday fully restore to Himself.

We do not, however, have to guess about God's love for us. God, himself, tells us He loves us when He spoke through the prophet Isaiah and said these beautiful words:

> *'Fear not, for I have redeemed you.*
> *I have summoned you by name; you are mine.*
> *When you pass through the waters, I will be with you.*
> *And when you pass through the rivers, they will not sweep over you.*
> *When you walk through the fire, you will not be burned; the flames*
> *will not set you ablaze.*
> *For I am the Lord, your God, the Holy One of Israel, your Savior…*
> *Since you are precious and honored in my sight,*
> *And because I love you…' (Isaiah 43:1-4)*

Perhaps the most meaningful evidence we have of God's love is found in the very recognizable John 3:16 verse, *For God so loved the world that He gave His only begotten son that whosoever should believeth in Him should not perish but have everlasting life.* (KJV)

At times in our earthly relationships, we are confused about love. If we don't feel it, does that mean we don't love? Should we push ahead with actions that show love, and hope the feelings follow? Many people just give up if they don't feel love, assuming they must not love. They fail to realize that while surface feelings can follow actions (we can feel happy after a fun celebration, for example), but true emotions follow our thoughts and precede our actions.

It makes sense, then, that in our humanness, we would have difficulty accepting God's love for us, much less understanding the depth and degree of His love. But it is there. It is all around us. It sustains us and fills us and allows us to love others in ways that God has prepared for us to do. His love works through us burdening our hearts for those around us. His love moves us to action!

From Reova's own journal and devotion she writes…

In the gospels, the teachers of the law ask Jesus which is the greatest commandment and Jesus answers, '*Love the Lord your God with all your heart and with all your soul and with all your mind and with all your strength*' Mark 12:30. This means that our love to God must come from all our inward affections (our heart), all our consciousness (our soul), all of our thoughts (our mind), and with all of our energy and power (our strength.)

So, how do we do that? How do we show God we are loving Him with everything that we are? First, we acknowledge Him as creator, yielding our minds. There is no other. We recognize that He and all His ways are perfect, yielding our hearts. We want nothing more. Then we accept that He loves us and reached down to save us, yielding our souls. Our lives are His. And finally, we listen and respond to what God says in His Word, yielding our will and our strength. I live to do your will.

When we love God, His Word becomes a shining light and guides our daily activities. But we must *know* God's Word… what it says, what it means, and how it applies to our daily lives.

In his book, Ruthless Trust, Brennan Manning writes, **"If we are having trouble trusting God at least one of two things is true:**

1. **We do not love God enough** or
2. **We do not know how much He loves us."**

When God led the children of Israel out of Egypt they had known God's deliverance, but they still murmured and complained – they hadn't yet learned His great love for them!

September 2001 – (After having this discussion with my high school friend, Winnie.) I'm lying here thinking about my discussion with Winnie. I had been telling her about my struggle with faith and Brennan Manning's words: "If we're having trouble trusting God one of two things is wrong, either we don't know how much He loves us or we don't love Him enough."

I told her I didn't feel I loved Him enough. She said, "I don't think we can love him as we should until we realize how much He loves us."

As I've been lying here awake, it seems to course through me - "God loves me so much".

Lord, help me to understand this and respond in love – I don't know how to live this love out so I can trust you like I want to be able to.

I'm sure one reason I'm having trouble understanding how much God loves me is because Dad never seemed to delight in me or approve of me. Doug didn't love and delight in me or approve of me. How can I understand how much God loves and delights in me if no one has modeled that in my life.

Lord, give me a revelation of this – The words that He said were: "Come away, my fair one." I got my Bible and began to read from Song of Solomon. Song of Solomon is a discourse between the lover and the beloved. I wrote down the words of the lover!

> *How beautiful you are, my darling!*
> *Oh, how beautiful!*
> *Your eyes behind your veil are doves...*
> *Your lips are like a scarlet ribbon;*
> *your mouth is lovely.*
> *Your temples behind your veil*
> *are like the halves of a pomegranate.*
> *Your neck is like the tower of David...*
> *You are altogether beautiful, my darling;*
> *there is no flaw in you...*
> *You have stolen my heart*
> *with one glance of your eyes. (Song of Solomon 4:1-9, excerpts)*

Then He gave me a personal message from Him:

"You are beautiful,
You are lovely,
You are treasured,
You are perfect,
I delight in you!
Let me wrap my arms around you.
Lay your head upon my breast and rest!
You don't need to worry about a thing,
I will take care of everything that concerns you."

The Lord has entered this basement bedroom here in Greeley CO and turned it into a bridal suite and showed me how much He loves me. Tonight, I feel like a bride being drawn into the arms of her lover – One whom I can trust to provide all I'll ever need. Protect me from all evil and allow only those things He deems "good" to come into my life to love, value and treasure me forever.

I've been reading Anne Graham Lotz' book *Vision of His Glory*, and she talks about the bride making herself ready for the bridegroom from Revelation 19. She says the bride's wedding garments are made of fine linen, bright and clean, representing the righteousness of the saints. She warns that some of us may look like we are only wearing a slip because while we are saved, we have lived for ourselves. While others will wear gowns fit for a princess with yards and yards of the finest linen because they have lived wholly for Christ.

My wedding gown cost $10.90 and was made of inexpensive satin covered with nylon netting. But I'm looking forward to the day when I stand before my heavenly groom and my gown will then be fit for a princess with yards and yards of the finest linen for the righteous acts of the saints because I have lived totally for Christ. And just like in the Song of Solomon 2:10, I will hear Him say, *Arise, my darling, my beautiful one, and come with me.*

Awake – March 1987

Last night I lay awake again for hours. I'm so burdened about a world out there that needs and wants Christ. I'm so troubled that I'm teaching kids to read and do math when lots of people could and would do that. I'm troubled that I see fighting, even in the church, over power, praise, and honor and that I'm tied to Doug with all his self-serving struggle. These things take all my energies when so many need what Christ has to offer and I could tell them if only I could be released from these things. Lord, help me to someway fulfill this burden to help others.

April 1987

You know the burden I have to help people become spiritual giants; give me an opportunity. In JoAnna Weaver's book, *Having a Mary Heart in a Martha World,* she says, "Intimacy with Jesus allows us to be: honest in our complaints, bold in our approach and lavish in our love. It is impossible to be in the presence of Jesus and not be changed"

If our girls really knew how much God loves them, healing would come!

Chapter Three

HOLY DISCONTENTMENT, LOSS, AND CHANGES

It was 1987 and Reova was active in her local church congregation, attending regularly, teaching a young adult Sunday School Class and available for whatever opportunities she was suited for. At home she was suffering in her marriage, constantly crying out to the Lord to help her deal with these difficulties, to show her how to be Christ-like, and how to make a difference for good amidst such turmoil.

At the same time, Reova began to feel unsettled at church. Her only place of solace outside her troubled marriage was now feeling like shaky ground. As is often the case, when God is preparing us for a task He has for us, we begin to feel a holy discontentment where we are serving. In His grace, He sometimes makes it easier for us to make a change. When a bigger Yes awaits, He helps us with the letting- go. At this point, Reova began to feel God's nudging toward a new ministry or something He was about to ask her to do. Still, the only joy she had left was teaching her young adult class, and she felt God was asking her to give that up! In her words...

> Another issue that required attention was me giving up the Sunday School class of young married couples that I had been teaching for several years. The members of the class weekly came to me for

counseling and advice. I argued with the Lord saying, "Who is going to counsel and advise them? Who is going to love them like I do and pray for them like I do?" The Lord's answer was, "Reova, they don't belong to you- they belong to me, and I will take care of them."

The next class session, I resigned. My words to the Lord were, "I'm ready for a wider ministry if you will take care of the issue I have in my home. That is the only hindrance between me and this ministry for which I feel you are preparing me.

The emotional pain that followed was so great that I cried for days with all the losses. I prayed, "It hurts so much even though I know this is the right thing. Lord, I have now relinquished everything dear to me. Open my life to wider service and ministry for you." Still, the pain continued, "I can't believe it can hurt so much when I know I'm doing what God wants. I've cried and cried – the hurt and loss is deeper than anything I've ever known. However, I'm convinced a new ministry is waiting and the Lord is clearing the way. Lord, someway heal this brokenness and loss I feel. Please help me to remain faithful."

When the first Sunday came that I did not teach my class, I wrote, "I'm feeling deep pain. I don't understand. All I know is I'm doing what God wants done by not teaching my class, but the pain and loss is tremendous. I thought healing had come but I was wrong. I guess it's so hard when I think how many Sunday School teachers did not want to teach this morning but did anyway, and here I'm hurting and struggling because I want to and can't.

During this time of not teaching my class the scripture in Joel 2:25-26 seemed to minister to me in a new way: *I will repay you for the years the locusts have eaten... You will have plenty to eat, until you are full, and you will praise the name of the Lord your God, who has worked wonders for you.*

After confessing to him my anger, resentment, bitterness and asking for forgiveness, I finally told the Lord, this is the last barrier between me and a new fruitful ministry. I'm ready now.

I felt so clean and emptied of hindrances – I've passed the test – I can come out of the desert.

Chapter Four

PREPARING FOR WHAT?

The days and months dragged on without any direction from God. Reova tried to listen for any word from God that might reveal to her what it was she was supposed to do next. Have you ever been there? It can be a silent, lonely time and requires staunch faith. It was not easy, and Reova felt herself wondering if she had heard God accurately. She felt certain things were changing in her heart, but she couldn't make it fit with nothing else happening. It all felt like a futile waste of time. In her words...

Thursday, Oct. 1, 1987

It seems so strange the last few mornings; Nothing is happening in my life spiritually. I learned so many lessons this summer but now I seem to be biding time. I'm finding it difficult to read the Bible or pray.

I still have a real urge to spend all my efforts helping people get to Heaven and live productive lives spiritually as they get there, but I don't seem to have any opportunities. All I'm doing is teaching school and waiting for something to happen. It's so hard just doing nothing. Lord, I long for action but help me wait patiently while you are preparing the way.

Sunday, October 4, 1987

I'm becoming more and more burdened over the drugs, sex, alcohol, in our world, perhaps the Lord is letting me become so concerned because this is part of my new world.

October 14, 1987

A friend gave me three butterfly magnets, not realizing how significant they are for my life right now. I wrote a note of thanks, "They are the result of a beautiful metamorphosis. That's what's been happening in my life. The last five months of being in solitude have been my chrysalis. During this time of hiding, darkness, waiting – a wonderful change takes place, preparing the butterfly for higher and more beautiful things. This I believe is happening to me. Waiting has been dreary. Inner changes have been severe and painful. The darkness has at times been rather scary, but I feel I'm about to emerge to a higher and more beautiful life.

October 16, 1987

I talked this morning to a woman whose sister died in a convent, her husband a terrible alcoholic, her daughter on drugs, her son attempted suicide, and her business went bankrupt. My struggle seemed minor compared to what she was dealing with. Still, I shared with her what's been happening in my life the last several months – about giving up the Sunday School class, the butterfly revelation, my summer spent in solitude, and my changed attitudes toward prayer and God. She said (and it was so reaffirming to hear), "The Lord is getting you ready for a wider ministry than that Sunday School class, Reova." I've believed that but oh how I needed the Lord to speak those words again through someone else. Thank you, Lord.

As we spoke a paper from her Bible fluttered to the floor. On it was written, "Wisdom is the mind of Christ in control of your life." As I drove home, almost three hours, it was a continual communion with God. I told Him how much I loved Him – couldn't love Him more unless He increases my capacity to love. I have an unhindered desire to serve Him and do His will. It couldn't be greater unless He can make it greater – right now I'm at full capacity in my Christian relationship to Christ. I feel like I am one with the Father. . .

> As He speaks, I speak
> As He moves, I move
> As He waits, I wait.

I'm not sure this expresses my feelings exactly but I'm having a hard time putting what's happening to me into words.

October 18, 1987

This morning, I feel so troubled over the slowness of nothing working out. I guess the devil has been at work as I slept. I really do want to be faithful. I feel the end is near and a break is about to take place. Lord, help me to wait.

Wednesday, October 28, 1987

This morning I'm finding it all just too much. I feel in my humanness that all the trusting, all the submission, all the learning of new spiritual lessons have been in vain. Five and a half months later nothing that I struggled with in May has changed. I used to feel I could predict what God was going to do and how He was working things out. Today, I guess He's trying to show me He'll do it His way and in His own time. I know all these things can be solved overnight – even in five minutes of time – when God gets ready. I'm certainly having trouble waiting for God to do something. It seems all the changes I've made have been to no avail. Right now, they've gotten me nowhere – but God understands.

November 18, 1987

I was thinking this morning, "It's been six months since the crisis broke. Nothing that troubled me then has worked out." Perhaps it's a greater miracle that the Lord changed me, rather than my situation.

Sun, Nov. 20, 1987

Struggling again why nothing is happening. I so want to be involved with something – so tired of nothing!

Sun. January 17, 1988

Another thought has come to me while I've been reading this morning – in fact the thought has surfaced before. "Maybe I'm still trying mentally to determine what God is going to do – how He is going to work out all the tangles of my life – when what He wants is me to mentally leave it all to Him and let Him do "exceedingly abundantly, above all we could ask or think."

Chapter Five

HE SPEAKS! AND, OH, WHAT HE SAYS!

During these years in the late 1980's, Reova was still a third grade school teacher with a Doctorate in Education. That's right. An elementary teacher with a doctorate! Her dream had always been to teach at the college level, but the right opportunity had not presented itself.

She was 3 years away from retirement when she felt God speaking to her about an entirely new direction for her life. In her words...

> Early in 1988, I was reading Isaiah 61:1-3; *The Spirit of the Sovereign Lord is on me, because the Lord has anointed me to proclaim good news to the poor. He has sent me to bind up the brokenhearted, to proclaim freedom for the captives and release from darkness for the prisoners, to proclaim the year of the Lord's favor and the day of vengeance of our God, to comfort all who mourn, and provide for those who grieve in Zion—to bestow on them a crown of beauty instead of ashes, the oil of joy instead of mourning, and a garment of praise instead of a spirit of despair.*
>
> It was as if the Lord drew a red mark around the words "to those who grieve in Zion" and was saying to me, "Reova, I'm preparing you for a new ministry that's going to reach beyond the influence of your local church, and it's going to be to 'those who grieve in Zion.'"

I didn't know what that meant or how I would be able to carry it out, or what the ramifications of it might be, but I knew that I had a directive from the Lord. Over the next few months, I continued to seek from the Lord what He wanted me to do, and He finally gave me this directive in three parts.

He said, *"First*, I want you to open a center of ministry for emotional and spiritual healing for women, and *second*, I want to use you as a catalyst to pull the Christian Community together in unity– not to be connected to any specific church, but an entity of your own. And *third*, I want to use you as an example of what I will do in response to obedience and truth."

I'm convinced in my heart today that if the Christian Community could understand what God would do in response to obedience and faith things would be a lot different in our world.

He also went on to say, "If you will do these things I will provide you with the money, the know-how, the people, and the materials to get this job done."

During this time Reova continued to struggle with questions and wonderings about what this ministry would look like and how it would operate, how she would lead it, and when it would happen! All the while she was seeking God earnestly, and He was molding her faith and her relationship with Him and growing her compassion for such a great need among women. In her words…

Friday, April 8, 1988

This morning in my devotions I was reading about Jesus' temptation when He rejected the swift fulfilment of His vocation presented to Him by Satan. I understand. I've been so tempted to rush into fulfillment of my vision of ministry to women and not wait God's timing. The devil's attack is to do God's will in our own way. This has been so true in my life. I pray I will be patient and wait for God's timing.

Monday, May 23, 1988

I feel so troubled this morning. Here I am still waiting, and things appear no nearer the end that they did months and months ago. I did what God asked me to do and I've constantly sought God's will. Right now, I need more strength to rest while I am waiting. Waiting is so hard.

Thursday, June 9, 1988

I went to a rape awareness workshop. There was a guy there who spoke up and said, "I was molested by a man in a mission in Indianapolis." He acted like he wanted to talk about it, and before the session was over he asked if there was anywhere in town where he could get help. But he left and walked out into the darkness before the session was over.

I feel such a burden for the hurting out there. All the agencies and groups in town are doing all they can but it's not enough. They don't have Christ. Christ is the answer!

Lord, continue to burn the idea of this Center for Women's Ministries on my heart and mind. Open up the way. You have all the financial resources and the manpower necessary to do this – show me the way.

Sunday, June 12, 1988

I am learning more lessons. I believe one thing God is teaching me is that it's all the same when we are in the center of God's will. Loss or gain, joy or sorrow. When we are in the center of God's will, it's all the same – what matters is being in His will.

Sunday, August 21, 1988

I heard a preacher say, that if we are truly obedient, then what's really important is how one act of disobedience affects God, not what the personal consequences are to ourselves. If obedience to God is not the primary goal – then what really matters – what we're really more concerned about is our own consequences. I believe I'm learning this 'contentment' lesson. I trust God and am leaving the consequences to Him. He's responsible for them, not me.

Another thing this preacher said is that God doesn't show the way. He only tells us to take the next step. The end He sometimes does not show us. Sometimes God makes us wait because we are not ready or prepared for the answer. Waiting is God preparing us for the answer. I'm being prepared. "Lord, help this part of me to be crucified so I can fully say, 'It doesn't matter who gets the credit – just so you get the glory." Maybe the reason it hurts so much is because I'm not involved in anybody's life right now and I want to be so badly. Lord, this growth is so painful."

Wednesday, September 7, 1988

I have a different kind of peace than I've had before. It seems I waited for God to work it all out but with an anxious spirit. My spirit has changed. I'm living each day trying to do His will but now I can leave the 'working out' to Him. The desire for change has not left but I have a calm contented peace like I've not had before. This is another step in growing in my dependency on God.

Sunday, September 18, 1988

The Lord gave me this scripture today: Acts 1:8 *But you will receive power when the Holy Spirit comes on you; and you will be my witnesses in Jerusalem, and in all Judea and Samaria, and to the ends of the earth.* I'm expecting my new ministry to reach beyond my church and Bloomington. I'm waiting for the power – and this is what is happening in my life.

Tues, September 20, 1988

I think the lesson I'm learning from the Lord now is how to be content in whatever state I'm in. I think the Lord is showing me that loss and gain, success and failure, desires met, and disappointments are all the same when we are in the center of His will. His will, no matter what, is all that matters. Lord, help me to rest in you in the center of your will!

Prayer

"In order to obey something God wants, it may mean giving up something we truly want. We should not expect obedience to God to be easy or always come naturally."

- REOVA MEREDITH

Chapter Six

WILL YOU OBEY?

Over the next months, this call from God became more clear and persistent. But so did another part of it. Starting a ministry seemed like a full-time job. And she already had one! In only three years she could collect retirement benefits. Could she wait? Should she wait?

She sensed the Lord's strong instruction that He meant **now**! In Reova's words...

Friday, May 16, 1989

I have been working on the details for retirement. I am three years short of full retirement. Retiring now will reduce my retirement benefits more than half. Since I bring in over half of our family income, this has become an issue with which to reckon. I had resigned before I left the last day of school but when I contacted the school retirement office for the official paperwork they tried to talk me out of the action telling me I could take a year's sabbatical, then come back for two years and teach two classes a day. I could then do the counseling ministry the rest of the day. Doing this still qualifies my job for the school system to carry my life insurance.

In the struggle of what decision to make concerning this I came across this scripture in Job 36:18. *Be careful that no one entices you with riches. Do not let a large bribe turn you aside.*

When I talked to the lawyer, he warned me about turning in my retirement papers – he felt it would be better to wait till things are farther along. He said, "I don't think the Lord expects you to 'saw off the limb under you' to prove your faith. I'm convinced of your faith by talking to you. You have brightened my day just by talking to you." I walked away from his office praying, "Lord, I need your direction about the retirement matter." The Lord challenged me, "Reova, are you trying to hold on to that job because you are afraid this will not work?" I had to answer 'yes'. There was simply so much at stake.

While I was struggling over this, I received these words in a letter from my son who had been reading *Spiritual Leadership* by J. Oswald Sanders. He quoted, "Once a spiritual leader is sure of the will of God, he will go into immediate action, regardless of the consequences. In pursuing his goal he will have the courage to burn his bridges behind him."

Finally, after three days I walked back into the retirement office and said, "I think you better give me those retirement papers." I have never questioned the wisdom of that decision nor been tempted to regret that choice.

Reova's current educational degree was a Doctorate, and her dream had always been to teach at the college level. Now that she had settled the matter about retiring and beginning this ministry full time, what do you think finally happened? In her words…

I had a Doctor's degree in Administration and Supervision in Education and my big goal was to be a college professor. I thought that was the most exciting, honoring thing I could do, and for 10 years I waited for that job, and it did not come.

But when I got ready to quit my job and leave the profession, I got a call from a Christian college, and they said they had two teacher education positions open and that I could have either one. The positions were exactly what I wanted - one in science and math, and the other one in social studies and language arts. So I went back to the Lord, trying to figure out how I could be this wonderful college professor, fulfilling this lifelong dream that I had, *and* do this ministry that the Lord had called me to do all at the same time.

After about 3 or 4 days of going back and forth in my mind with this, the Lord said to me, "Reova, I've taught you too much about living the Christian life for you to spend the rest of your life teaching teachers how to teach!"

I'm convinced that once we decide to do what God asks us to do, Satan will bring in an opportunity or a temptation that is so great it is hard to resist. I know Satan wouldn't bring a temptation for me to go out into outright sin. I was living close enough to the Lord that he knew that wasn't the way he could tempt me. But he could take the thing that was the dearest to my heart, and put that in front of me, and say, "Here it is - you can do this if you want to now."

After I dealt with that and refused that position, the ministry began to really unveil in my mind. It became clear exactly what the Lord wanted me to do. I believe that for all of us, there comes a time in our lives when we can be very easily sidetracked from doing God's will. There wasn't anything wrong with me going and teaching at a Christian College. There wasn't anything wrong with me preparing teachers to teach, but the Lord had something else He wanted me to do, and I believe He used Satan's temptation to test me on the area that was the dearest to my heart.

Obedience – The Most Rewarding Action
The Evidence of Love

In John 14:15 Jesus says, *If you love me, keep my commands.* It really can't be any simpler than that. The Christian life might be observed in the world by our words or actions or even our finances, but the true evidence of a genuine life in Christ is measured by God by one thing only - obedience.

The most interesting thing about obedience is that no one, not any other person on earth, can know for sure if we are being obedient to God, aside from God Himself. Oh, we might know if someone is not obeying the Ten Commandments or refusing to help the poor or needy, but when it comes to specific tasks set before us to fulfill God's purpose or plan for our individual lives…? No one else knows. That is between us and God. Kinda scary, huh?

Reova knew her whole life was dedicated to God and her love for Him began at such an early age. It would have been enough for her to share that part of her story, and we would have been none the wiser. Thankfully, her struggles with obedience are a part of this story for all to see and learn from. From her devotion…

OBEDIENCE

Obedience is the natural outflow of love. We may not always understand why God is asking us to do a particular thing. Often we probably won't understand why! The *why* is not important. We need only to understand who is speaking. And God, in His infinite knowledge and wisdom… He knows why! And that should be good enough for us with our finite knowledge and wisdom. We don't need to understand, we just need to obey – Obedience first – understanding later. Some commands we only understand as we obey. Some commands we may never understand in this lifetime. In his book, *My Utmost for His Highest,* Oswald Chambers says, "Obedience precedes the promise. By obedience we see who God is. The promises of God are of no value to us until by obedience we understand the nature of God."

In Genesis 6:22, Noah obeyed God completely. No instruction was overlooked. It says, *Noah did everything, just as God commanded him*. He also obeyed exactly regarding God's way and timing. *And Noah did all that the Lord commanded him*. Gensis 7:5.

Later in Gensis (26:4-5), God promises to bless Israel and the descendants because Abraham obeyed. *I will make your descendants as numerous as the stars in the sky and will give them all these lands... because Abraham obeyed me and did everything I required of him.*

Max Lucado once said, "Understanding is not essential. Obedience is!" After the disciples had been out fishing all night and not caught one single fish, Jesus sees them and tells them to let their nets down on the other side of the boat. I imagine their first thought may have been "He doesn't think we have already tried that?" But Luke tells us their response was, *Because you say so I will*. Luke 5:5

In his book, *Prayer*, Richard Foster said "Obedience has a way of strengthening rather than depleting our resources. If we obey in one small corner, we will have power to obey elsewhere. Obedience begets obedience."

I am not talking about an obedience with a martyr or self-pity attitude that says, "Well, I've been obedient, so God owes me this..." We must have a higher level of obedience with an attitude of thanksgiving and joy as in spiritual worship. This obedience is done out of love and gratitude for God, feeling that God owes me nothing! It is the test of the depth of a personal relationship with The Lord.

Sister Teresa of Avila once said, "The ability to bring our will into conformity with the will of God is the greatest thing we can accomplish on our spiritual journey."

But the end result of that obedience is a deeper, clearer understanding of God's love for us and our love for Him. When we are obedient to God, we are really saying, "I love you."

We need only to look at the stories of the sheep and their shepherd to see this example in scripture. John 10: 3-4 tells us, *The sheep listen to his voice. He calls his sheep by name and leads them out... and the sheep follow him because they know his voice.* There is a deep relationship of love and protection established that causes the sheep to obey. Their obedience is a product of the faithfulness of the shepherd. The sheep had only to OBEY.

In the 23rd Psalm we see that:

1. The shepherd is responsible to make them lie down in green pastures, in safety, rest, and peace. The sheep had only to OBEY.
2. The shepherd is responsible to lead them beside still waters and provide them with life-giving water. The sheep had only to OBEY.
3. The shepherd is responsible to protect them - They were to fear no evil. The sheep had only to OBEY.
4. The shepherd would be with them for protection, encouragement, and discipline. The character, health and safety of the sheep are products of the shepherd's faithfulness. The sheep had only to OBEY and follow.

Does that mean obedience will be easy or without struggle? Without temptation to give up? No, it is often a struggle. In order to obey something God wants; it may mean giving up something we truly want. We should not expect obedience to God to be easy or always come naturally. It is our nature to question, to want the whole story and want assurances that everything will work out before we commit to anything. It is our nature to ask first and trust only after we have the answers we want. It is our nature to only trust ourselves first. That is what God asks us to give up – trust in ourselves (which often doesn't go according to plan because we can't know what lies ahead.) Trading our trust in self for trust in Him as we respond in obedience. Proof of our faith and trust is in our actions – our obedience.

The message of Hebrews 11, known as the Faith chapter, highlights the *actions* of faith 16 times as various stories are told. The ACTION is always **obedience.** Obedience to God – our actions, not our feelings, is proof of our trust in God.

We trust Him, and He is responsible for the results. Obedience places the responsibility on God. If we are really responsive to God's will and He reveals that it is His will that an actual mountain be removed, then we will quite literally be able to cast it into the sea, as in Mark 11. Nothing he wants done will be impossible! Now that doesn't mean that anything we attempt in our own initiative will be possible. But every God-prompted and God-initiated project is possible. Nothing is impossible that God tells us to do.

In his book, *The Fire of God's Love*, Bob Sorge writes, "God doesn't ask us to be creative but to be obedient. He says, 'Wait on Me until I speak to you!' It's easier to be creative than obedient. It's easier to press ahead with my own thoughts, than to wait on God for His thoughts."

Not only is obedience proof of our faith and trust, as we are obedient, we have hope, because we have done our part and can trust God to do His part. To hear His voice we must wait – but when we hear His voice – It's worth the wait!! **We must hear from God! Let's wait for His voice, then move ahead in obedience. Obedience is the sign of LOVE.**

I want to be able to say with the writer of Deut. 26:14, *I have obeyed the Lord my God. I have done everything you commanded me.*

OBEDIENCE

"We approach boldly with confidence because we know we are coming (by request) before the King of Kings and Lord of Lords – the Almighty God – with whom nothing is impossible."

— Reova Meredith

Chapter Seven

AN INTERESTING VISION AND LOTS OF PRAYER

Reova's words…

After the day that I quit my job, I had a vision. The vision was of a building with a tall steeple and short sides, and over the door of that building it said, "Center for Women's Ministries." For about 3 or 4 days I ran around all over Bloomington trying to find a similar-looking building. I finally realized that what God had given me was the name for the ministry: "Center for Women's Ministries".

Later when we were applying for the trademark registering our name and our logo, the name was denied the first time. So, we appealed and applied again, and I told the girls in the office, "I know it's going to pass because that's what the Lord gave me!" And the second time through it did pass, and we are the "Center for Women's Ministries."

Sometime later I began to build this pink file folder that said "Center for Women's Ministries" on it. Anything that would come to my mind- a scripture, a person I could talk to, or anything that might help- I put in that in the pink file folder. One day I was at the figure salon (as ladies used to call "the gym"), I was going through my last bicycle set and the Lord said, "You need to go to the north side of town and look at this building that used to be the Chamber of Commerce and now houses The Visitors' Bureau.

So I drove there and pulled in the parking lot of this building, and all the emotions inside of me just broke loose and I started crying. I pulled my car in and got out of the car, and I looked all around the empty building, and I knew in my heart this was where I needed to open the Center. I took down the number of the realtor and stuck it in my pink file folder and waited for the Lord to tell me when I could talk to this person. After about 3 weeks one day, I felt I should call him. He met me there and took me through the building. I told him this was like a dream in my mind because I had no money for this building. He told me when I had a more definite plan (and money) to give him a call.

Sometime after my initial experience of pulling in the parking lot of 'that' building, I received a phone call asking, "Have you done anything about the building?" I said 'no.' The reply was, "I heard as of next week, it's leased for a year."

I panicked on the inside. The devil immediately stole my peace. My mind began to say, "What are you going to do now? You've told others this is the building in which to start, you felt so sure about this. How can you have spiritual credibility about this thing if you are wrong? You told your co-workers the Lord is going to work this out, when they questioned the wisdom of you giving up your teaching position. Now you're in the process of preparing your teaching possessions to leave at the end of the school year. How does this defeat look on you?"

I had to breathe a prayer and remind myself, "Lord, this is not my project, but yours. I have nothing to win or lose." I looked up Joshua 1:11 in the Living Bible. *We will go across and conquer and live in the land which God has given us.* I guess I wasn't so 'tied' to the building as I was my credibility with the Lord in the eyes of others if we don't get this building. My prayer became "Lord, help me to be able to hand even that over to you."

The Lord gave these scriptures as wonderful reassurance:

Joshua 1:3 KJV *Every piece that the soul of your foot shall tread upon, that have I given you.*
Joshua 1:6 TLB *Be strong and brave, for you will be a successful leader.*
Joshua 1:6 TLB *Be strong and brave for you will be a successful leader of my people.*
Joshua 3:7 TLB *I will give you great honor, so that all will know that I am with you.*

I had repeatedly driven my car to the building, parked in the second spot east of the building, read my Bible, prayed for guidance, and given the entire situation to the Lord. Day after day, the building remained vacant.

For the next 14 months I took my Bible and my journal, and I went back to that building and pulled in that same parking lot every week and prayed about this ministry that I felt God wanted me to put in this building. One Sunday afternoon a friend of mine and I picked up a cup of coffee and decided to go to "The Center" to talk. We drove there and parked in that very same spot and spent about 3 hours talking and crying and praying.

Before we left, I looked up and there was a man standing at my car door. I had seen a van in the parking lot and someone doing some landscaping, but I didn't pay any attention to it. He asked, "Are you women here just trying to get yourselves together?"

I said, "Well, I've been watching this building now for over a year and I want to put a Center for Women's Ministries in it. What relationship do you have to the building?"

He said, "I'm the owner. I'm here from Florida until I get tenants in this building." So, I made an appointment with him, and in a couple of weeks, I had a lease for a portion of that building for $1500 a month besides utilities.

Prayer – The Most Powerful Channel of Communication

Two important scriptures concerning prayer bring with them at once encouragement and challenges. Hebrews 4:16 says, *Let us then approach God's throne of grace with confidence, so that we may receive mercy and find grace to help us in our time of need.* And Philippians 4:6 says, ***Do not be anxious about anything** but in every situation, by prayer and petition, with thanksgiving, present your requests to God.*

We are to come before God with confidence and then have no anxiety or worry about what will happen. Sounds easy enough… hardly! When we realize, however, *why* God is asking us to approach boldly with confidence and then not to worry, it's a little easier to get there. We approach boldly with confidence because we know we are coming (by request) before the King of Kings and Lord of Lords – the Almighty God – with whom nothing is impossible. And when we realize that not only is nothing impossible with Him, but His love and His plans for us are perfect and in our best interest, then why would we ever worry or be anxious? But we do!

What God was asking of Reova seemed totally impossible in every way. Financially, she was quitting her job ahead of retirement, she no longer had the youthful advantages of being in her twenties or thirties, and He was asking her to begin a ministry outside her educational background. You can't get much more impossible than that. If this was going to happen, it would have to be all God. From Reova's devotion on Prayer…

There was a man in Bristol, England in the 1800's named George Müller. He was a Christian evangelist and the director of the Ashley Down orphanage and a founder of the Plymouth Brethren movement. During his lifetime, he cared for over 10,000 orphans, opened 117 Christian schools, educating more than 120,000 children. It is said that Müller read the entire Bible more than 200 times, often on his knees. When asked how much time he spent in prayer, George replied, "Hours every day. But I live in the spirit of prayer. I pray as I walk, when I lie down and when I arise. And the answers are always coming."

Prayer has been so important in my life. We must believe that God hears and answers our prayers. Two scriptures I have come to rely on are II Chron. 7:15 that says, *Now my eyes will be open and my ears attentive to the prayers offered in this place,* and Jeremiah 29:12 where God says, *You will call upon me and come and pray to me and I will listen to you.*

Thomas Keating, a modern-day Catholic priest who wrote extensively on prayer, once said, "The only way to fail in prayer is to not show up."

I love an old story I once read in *Streams in the Desert,* by Mrs. Charles E. Cowman. She told of a Christian who dreamed she saw three people kneeling in prayer before the Lord. He stopped at the first one, speaking gently for quite a long time, the second, only pausing to touch her head for a brief moment, and the third, He seemingly passed by not stopping at all. The woman watching thought, "How deeply and surely He must love the first one; He approved the second, but the third must have grieved His heart deeply, for He hardly gave her a passing glance!"

As The Lord stood before her, he explained to her that the first woman needed His physical and tangible touch for she was vulnerable and at risk of losing her way. Meanwhile, the second woman's faith was more mature, and she was learning to truly trust Him. But surprisingly, He was training the third woman for a high and holy calling. She knew Him intimately and no longer depended on outward signs of His approval. Of the third woman The Lord said, "She is not swayed and is satisfied to wait for all explanations until later, for she knows whom she has believed."

The more time we spend with Him in prayer, the surer we become of what is and what is not His will!

Author, Pastor, and Theologian, J. Sidlow Baxter said,

> "Men may spurn our appeals,
> Reject our messages,
> Oppose our arguments,
> Or Despise our persons,
> But they are helpless against our prayer."

And Charles Spurgeon once said, "It is the strength and not the length of your prayer that brings an answer to your prayers; the strength of prayer lies in your faith in the promise which you pleaded before the Lord."

June 1989

I had taken the lease to the lawyer that had drawn up our incorporation papers and left them with him to look over. A couple days later, I went back, and he said, "Reova, this lease is fine but I need to talk to you. I'm really concerned about what you're doing. He took me into the conference room where we sat at this very intimidating legal table. He looked at me and said, "Do you have any idea how much money you are committing to if you rent this building?"

"Oh yes, I know!" I said. "I'm committing to $1,500 a month, $18,000 a year, for at least $36,000 because I'm signing a two-year lease."

He looked at me and said, "How much money do you have in the bank?"

"Well," I answered, "After I pay out this $1,500 now I'll have $634."

"And that doesn't include any utilities. You are only paying for one month's access to the building to get it ready to open?"

"Yes, that's right." I hadn't put a desk in there. I hadn't put any chairs in there. I hadn't put anything in that building, and all I had was $634.

"And you're quitting your job to do this?"

"Yes."

"Do you think that's wise?"

"No", I had to admit. "But this is what I feel like God's asking me to do." Looking back now, I still don't know how I had the courage to quit my job with very little backing for this huge task. I had maybe $50 a month promised to me toward this ministry which certainly didn't seem wise in the human sense.

"I just feel like this is what I'm supposed to do, and I have to do it." So I picked up my lease and I walked out, and I hardly got through the front door before Satan was right there on my shoulder whispering in my ear. "You know you can't do this, and you're going to be a failure, and you're going to be a fool." Then he reminded me of a conversation I had with Dick, the landlord and owner of the building. Dick had told me that his banker was not the least bit supportive of our endeavor. His banker told him, "This is the most foolish move you've ever made, to rent her this space, because she'll never stay. She won't be able to pay your rent, and you're supposed to be a smart businessman!"

Satan reminded me of that conversation, and again, I had to admit it all sounded so foolish. But then I said, "Lord I didn't quit my job to be a failure, and I didn't quit my job to be a fool, but I'll be a fool for you because I will be obedient."

Something was settled that moment because it was total commitment and a total pouring out of myself. I realized I couldn't do any of this by myself and I was completely and wholly dependent on God. I walked out of the lawyer's office crying my eyes out. But before I got out of that parking lot, I had settled something with the Lord. This was totally His ministry, and I would be obedient, but He had to make it all happen. It was settled.

June 1989

When I got ready to sign the lease, the Lord gave me Philippians 4:16 *Do not be anxious about anything **but in every situation**, by prayer and petition, with thanksgiving, present your requests to God.* I'm claiming that scripture for the remodeling work that needs to be done at the location.

And I've had so much terror in my heart about contacting other community leaders about providing leadership for this ministry, but the Lord gave these scriptures:

Psalm 56:3- *When I am afraid, I put my trust in you.*
Isaiah 12:2 *I will trust and not be afraid.*
Jeremiah 1:8, 9- *You must go to everyone I send you to and say whatever I command you. Do not be afraid of them, for I am with you and will rescue you," declares the Lord.*
Jeremiah 33:2, 3 *Call to me and I will answer you and tell you great and unsearchable things you do not know.*
Hebrews 13:6 - So we say with confidence, *"The Lord is my helper; I will not be afraid. What can mere mortals do to me?"*

What encouraging promises!

June 15, 1989

This morning if I'd go by my feelings, I'd just quit trying to put this center together. It's just too big a job. Sometimes

I wonder if I know what I'm doing! Pastor said, during the Sunday morning message, "When we're serving God, we're serving a specialist in every field." Lord, I need a specialist in organizing this new ministry – send me someone who knows how to do this.

I'm saying, "Lord, I can't do this – I can't do this." But it's as if the Lord is saying, "Reova, I don't want you to do this. I want to do it." Here's something I've just been reading from Oswald Chambers, "We may face situations beyond our reserves, but never beyond God's resources."

Another quote I've run across from someone: "What God calls us to do is always impossible, impossible without His help. It is always too big for us; we must depend on Him."

God gave me these scriptures during this emotional time of uncertainty:

Isaiah 57: 14-15-" *Remove the obstacles out of the way of my people." For this is what the high and exalted One says—he who lives forever, whose name is holy.*
Psalm 44:3- *It was not by their sword that they won... it was your right hand, your arm.*
Exodus 36:2- *And Moses called . . . every skilled person to whom the Lord had given ability and who was willing to come do the work.*
Exodus 36:7- *And the people brought more than enough to do the work the Lord commanded to be done.*
I Chronicles 12:22 - *Day after day men came to help David, until he had a great army, like the army of God.*
Jeremiah 15:19 - *If you utter worthy, not worthless, words, you will be my spokesman.*
Zechariah 4:6- *Not by might nor by power, but by my Spirit,' says the Lord Almighty.*
Luke 21:15- *For I will give you words and wisdom that none of your adversaries will be able to resist or contradict.*

Chapter Eight

PREPARATIONS AND MORE PRAYER!

From an observer's perspective, it would seem things were falling into place, and the vision God had given Reova to open a Center for Women's Ministries where hurting women could find help and hope was coming to fruition. But so many things still needed to be done and Reova was no closer to knowing the next step than she was the step before. God was unfolding His plan one page at a time, keeping Reova desperately waiting for His next instruction. She clung to the promise she had received that God would provide the people, the resources, and the know-how as she laid out the needs before Him. In her words...

People

The scripture references the Lord sent me to as I thought about the people needed to make the ministry successful are from I Chronicles 12:22: *Men came to David to help him, until there was a great army.* Verse 32: *Men who understood the times, with knowledge of what Israel should do.* And verse 38: *The rest were also of one mind.*

Verse 22 meant that God would send me everyone I needed. Verse 32 meant the people He sent would understand what this community needed and how the Center could meet those needs. Verse 38 meant the people He sent would be Christians.

I began to pray, "Lord, you know where the right people are. Help me find them and become so powerful selling this ministry that they can't refuse." When I began to feel it was time to approach the professionals for the Board of Directors, the Lord gave me Acts 1:8AMP *But ye shall receive power and ability when the Holy Spirit has come upon you.* I felt so vulnerable and insecure when thinking of approaching the professionals.

This struggle seemed to recur when it was time to contact a local influential lawyer I felt should be on the Board of Directors. I sent him an outline of our organizational plan and asked for an appointment. One afternoon as I was out walking, his wife, a fellow teacher, stopped me. We talked of my plans for retirement, an update on the progress of the Center and told her of my plan to ask her husband to be on the Board. Before we parted, she said, "Reova, there are a lot of people out there supporting you." That was good to hear when sometimes you feel you are alone in this.

A couple of weeks later, following a real struggle of fears and doubts, I went to talk to the lawyer. I told my story of personal spiritual preparation and what had happened so far with the Center. He said, with tears in his eyes, "Reova, I first want to say, you have certainly brightened my day. You are very powerful when you tell this story." My heart said, "Thank you, Lord." I'd been asking the Lord to make me powerful as I told the story. Isn't it just like God to prompt this man to use the same word in describing as I had used in my prayer? God is so affirming!

He continued, "I believe in what you are doing. How can I help?" When I told him I'd like him to be on the Board of Directors, he said, "Sure, I'd like to." The devil made it look so hard, but the Lord prepared the way.

Building and Furnishings

I went through each room of the center praying and asking for everything we needed specifically.

My office:
desk and credenza and chair
sofa and chair
carpet and wall covering
window coverings

Office:
computer
desk
typewriter
chairs
carpet,
wall covering
41 new ceiling tiles

Lounge:
carpet for room and stairs
sofa
3 chairs
coffee table
lamps
tables
wall covering

Snack area:
floor covering
wall coverings
table and chairs

Kitchenette:
floor and wall coverings
Library:
bookshelves
table
chairs
wall covering

Counseling rooms:
5 sofas
5 chairs
5 tables
4 lamps

Meditation Chapel:
carpet
worship center seating
wall covering

I also asked the Lord for $100,000 before opening day. The lawyer said I needed a year's budget in the bank before I opened. I had made out a budget that included salary for the director, office manager, rent, utilities and phone. At that point I did not know God's plan for this to be an all-volunteer organization.

I prayed specifically for these. The Lord has promised to provide for our needs. He promised it would come when we needed it. I am approaching the throne of grace with confidence and without fear as it says in Hebrews 4:16.

As I prayed, I just felt the power of God arise in my being. I got out of my chair and began to walk with my arm uplifted carrying my Bible. I asked for a capacity to trust God more. I sensed in a new way this is the word of God and I could trust Him to fulfill His word. "Thank you, Lord, for a new revelation of your power and that we really can trust you and you won't let us down. I know I still haven't adequately expressed this experience. It was so powerful, such a realization, I can trust God. He IS trustworthy and will not go back on His word.

I began to praise Him with the words of this old hymn:

> "Tis so sweet to trust in Jesus
> Just to take Him at His word
> Just to rest upon His promise
> Just to know "Thus saith the Lord."

It's so hard to believe we can really take God at His word and know He will do it! I've been asking Him to help me trust Him more. "Increase my capacity to trust you Lord!" Back to Hebrews 4:16 AMP ...*grace to help in time of need [an appropriate blessing, coming just at the right moment].* Thank you, Lord, for restoring my soul in you. Psalm 23:2, *He refreshes my soul,* has taken on a new meaning.

Painting:

There were eleven rooms that needed to be painted. A week before the carpet was scheduled to be installed, only two of those rooms had been painted. I cannot paint. It doesn't matter how careful I try to be, the paint always ends up on my elbows, so I knew this was something I simply could not do.

Sunday morning, I was struggling emotionally, physically, and spiritually. I went for a walk around our country mile. About halfway around I literally threw up my hands and said, "Lord, you know I can't paint and if this painting never gets done, I have to quit losing sleep over it and stop worrying about it."

I received a call the next morning from the jail telling me they had heard I needed painters. On Tuesday, Wednesday, Thursday, and Friday, they sent five community restitution workers and by 5:00 pm on Friday the building was ready for carpet! Only God!

August 18, 1989

Right now I am so burdened for the center. Dedication is ten weeks away. The building is not finished – we're waiting for the drywallers to get their work done. No money is coming in. I don't seem to know what to do about furniture and stuff to redecorate the building. Everything seems overwhelming. Sometimes I want to crawl back to the comforts and safety of the cocoon. It's less risky, less chance for injury and hurt. But I've rid myself of all I have any control over – organizational involvement, Sunday School class, excessive clothes, job, - now the rest is up to you. I have no control over the rest. Lord, this is your project, and you gave me such an affirmation with this promise when I was so troubled saying: 'Lord, I can't do this – I can't do this' you said, "Reova, I don't want you to do this. I want to do it." Lord, help me to back off and let you do it.

In addition to getting the building ready, Reova and her faithful volunteers spent countless hours preparing the curriculum they would use to train other volunteers to counsel. Months of research and writing were headed up by dedicated volunteers and finally a usable training came to fruition. God had His hand in every single part of it and just as He promised, He provided the right people with the right skills at the right time. In Reova's words...

Know How

Since directing a 'center' and counseling others is not the profession my formal training prepared me to do, I have an ever-increasing need to constantly seek wisdom from the Lord. Someone adequately stated, "Wisdom is the mind of God in control of your life."

I remind the Lord constantly we can't afford to made 'big' mistakes in this ministry. We might survive some 'small' errors, but the work we are doing is far too important to make 'big' mistakes.

Many times I've returned to James 1:5 *If any of you lacks wisdom, he should ask God, who gives generously to all. . . and it will be given him.* Only recently did I discover the verse following in the Living Bible translation. *When you ask Him, be sure that you really expect Him to tell you, for a doubtful mind will be unsettled... and every decision you then make will be uncertain* James 1:6 TLB. I'm learning by experience that after you have prayed, believing God for wisdom, you can trust your instincts. Verse 8 says, *If you don't ask with faith, don't expect the Lord to give you any solid answer* James 1:8 TLB.

Satan has tried to convince me there is no way a fledgling ministry can prosper and be successful, but I claim the promise Joshua 1:6 *Be strong and brave for you will be a successful leader of my people.* Also, Jeremiah 33:3 *Call to me and I will answer you and tell you great and unsearchable things you do not know.*

My continued prayer became: "Lord, make me a woman of prayer and faith and give me wisdom and discernment that I might be successful in the work to which you have called me.

Repeatedly I've had to asked God for "know how". I read in *God Calling*, Sept 17, "Put all fear of the future aside. Know you will be led. Know that you will be shown. I have promised."

August 20, 1989

The Lord sent volunteers to counsel, facilitate Bible Studies and support groups, keep the books, cover the phone and other clerical chores, set up and oversee the library, provide custodial cleaning on a regular basis and a group of prayer warriors to undergird all our activities with prayer. One volunteer offered her home to serve as emergency housing for girls who needed to leave their present living situation. Four days after her offer a desperate young mother and four-year-old son moved into this dear obedient lady's home.

Materials and Furnishings

The building was finally beautifully decorated and furnished. I told the Lord I wanted new 'stuff', not what had been sitting in someone's basement for years. Our furnishings were virtually all new donations. Much of our building was wallpapered. We have been asked, "Who is your interior decorator?" Our reply had been, "When we are serving God, we're serving a specialist in every field."

One of the volunteers, who had such a vision for the ministry, had been sending us what was left over from her weekly grocery money. She felt she should approach a friend of hers who owned an appliance store. She told them about the ministry, and they donated a color TV and VCR for the library. Then over lunch one day she told them the fire code prevents us from having a stove. They responded with, "You could use a microwave, couldn't you?" They showed her an Amana microwave and told her we could have it at cost when we found someone to donate it. Before nightfall she found a donor who said, "I've been wanting to do something for the Center but didn't know what to do. Here's my answer!" And she happily paid for the microwave.

There was a grandmother who had been instrumental in securing donations for furnishings for the Center who was now looking for a couch and loveseat. Ten days before the open house, she felt impressed to go a shop that makes custom furniture. They had a couch in mauve and said they could make the love seat in a week if they had 13 yards of fabric left from the couch. They measured and there were 13 ½ yards left. The owner said he needed an

$85.00 deposit. She had $86.00 and some change in her wallet. When her husband found out about the purchase, he said he would pay for the couch and love seat.

How the lounge went together is remarkable. Different people presented each of the following (without consultation): love seat, couch, chairs, lamp tables, mirrors, and wallpaper. All of it looked like a professional had designed it.

A custom cabinet maker measured our kitchenette and presented beautiful cabinets as a gift. The G.E. factory donated a top-of-the-line refrigerator. A small table and four chairs were also donated for the snack area.

The story of the furniture for my office is incredible. My family decorated and furnished the director's office. One of my sisters, whose husband is a minister, promised to buy my desk. She began to think about what she had promised and said, "Lord, a desk could cost $600. Where am I going to get $600 for that desk?" Her husband went to a factory that manufactured new desks and asked if they had any "seconds." The plant manager "I have one and a matching credenza that were $1328 each retail. You may have them for $200 each." As they talked about the Center and its' ministry, the manager said, "In that case, you may have them for $50.00 each." When we went to pick them up, they had a matching bookcase which he put on the truck for $30.00. As I discussed with the factory manager how excited I was about the furniture, he said, "It's very unusual I get two pieces back from freight that match. Several people have looked at those pieces, but no one took them." I said, "Well, they were waiting for us I guess." He replied, "That's how God works, isn't it?" A few weeks later from that same factory we received an L-shaped secretary's desk for $200.00.

We secured side chairs for offices, the lounge, counseling rooms, and library from a chair factory that had cleared out their show rooms and put the chairs in storage for quick sell. Chairs that were priced retail over $200.00 we bought for $40.00 each.

A local chiropractor in her mid-30s developed a real hunger to know God in a personal way. Not knowing where to go, she went to the public library seeking a book that would help her find God. The only thing she found was a book entitled, *The City of God*. She discovered it to be an interesting novel but no help in her spiritual quest. Later, after finding God as her personal Savior, she went back to the public library, offering to buy $400 worth of books to be set aside in a collection to help people find God. The library refused her offer, so she said, "I'll provide $400 worth of books for your library." So this dear lady, our librarian, and I met at the local Christian bookstore and selected the books together for our library. This generous gift was a real boost to the resources of an 'infant' media center.

One of the volunteers put me in contact with a local graphic designer who was opening his new business. His first question was, "What is your budget for graphics? I stumbled, not knowing how to respond. I had very little money, and no budget for graphic arts. He continued probing, "How much do you plan to spend for this work?" When I couldn't answer that question, he finally told me his jobs usually run between $800 and $1500. I told him I felt it was a waste of his time for us to meet. I could not pay that. Then he said, "I'd still like to hear about your ministry, so let's meet." After he heard about what we are doing, he decided to do the LOGO for $85.00 and design everything else – brochures, envelopes, stationery, and business cards for $85.00, total - $170.00 - $1000 worth of artwork for $170.00!

The small roughly painted sign to our entrance of the building was destroyed by vandals and the post put into our mailbox. One of the girls in a support group asked, "What about your sign?" I replied, "I don't have the money to replace it so I'm just waiting." She said, How about letting me take care of it." In a couple of weeks she brought in an outdoor sign, a duplicate stationary imprint with exact colors, lettering, and logo. It had been professionally prepared. I couldn't help but think of the words of Joseph in Genesis 50:20 *You intended to harm me, but God intended it for good to accomplish what is now being done, the saving of many lives.*

Donations continued to arrive, filing cabinet, typewriters, copier, pamphlet display rack, folding chairs, sweeper, love seats for the counseling rooms, toys for the children's playroom, blinds, curtains, Bibles, library books and tapes, as well as all kitchen, cleaning, and paper consumables.

A week before the Open House, when it appeared there was still no way the building would be ready, cleaning would be finished, and the furnishings would be in place. But as if by miracle, volunteers began to descend on the Center, papering walls, cleaning windows, bringing in furnishings, and putting the fishing touches in place. One volunteer said to his wife the eve of Open House, "Reova has seen her first miracle – the building is ready!"

Chapter Nine

THE RESULT OF OBEDIENCE – THE CENTER FOR WOMEN'S MINISTRIES FINALLY OPEN!

After all of the praying and crying and preparing, the opening of the Center finally happened! As in the beginning of anything, there were still kinks to iron out. Clients needed appointments and schedules needed arranged. But all in all, the dream had been realized – at least the beginning of it. The training was written, the volunteers had been trained, the walls were painted, and the doors were opened. Reova could honestly say she had been obedient and seeing the Center finally open for counseling was the result of her obedience.

Why do we always seem to think that when we follow God's directions it will result in no more troubles? We tend to expect that since God can do anything and He has given us a task – to which we have been obedient- we can walk through the doors of peace and contentment, kick our feet up and enjoy the results, over and done!

Reova often remembered the directives she received from the Lord. He had told her to do three things; First, open a center of ministry for emotional and spiritual healing for women. Check! Second, be a catalyst to pull the Christian Community together in unity. Check (in progress!) And third, be an example of what I will do in response to obedience and truth. Check!

And He promised four things in response to her obedience. He promised to provide the money, the know-how, the people, and the materials for all He was asking her to accomplish.

For sure God had been faithful to provide so many people to support, help and walk alongside her during the start of the ministry. He had been faithful to provide the know-how and the materials and all the many resources in miraculous ways. So naturally, Reova wholeheartedly believed God would also provide the money. And He did, and He has. Only not in the ways Reova anticipated. To us, God's provisions should look like a bulky bank account when the bills come due… every single time the bills come due… month after month after month. Afterall, doesn't He own the cattle on a thousand hills? Aren't all of the reserves in His coffers always full?

Turns out, not only does He have endless supplies of whatever resources we need, He also has endless ways to keep His promises. He is much more creative than our near-sighted, anxiety-ridden monthly patterns of bill-paying. *And…* He also has lessons for us to learn along the way. He's not sweating when the rent comes due. He *has* the money. He sees the solution before the next month ever comes. He is much more concerned with our response to an empty bank account and much more concerned with our trust in Him than the empty bank account itself. While we are pacing and wringing our hands and crying out, He is simply saying, "My child! I see. I know. I'm fully aware. I have ways to help you. And besides, nothing in all the world can keep you away from what I have prepared for you here one day when this is all over!"

Reova's miracle experience of find the building and meeting the landlord would never dim. But it would become years of an internal struggle over empty bank accounts nearly every single time the rent came due. In spite of these struggles, God was still at work… in her heart, in the ministry, and in every person involved. In her words…

March 5, 1990

I've been thinking about the struggles of my life, including the fact that the Center seems to have continual financial struggles, and the last two weeks we have had limited activity as far as clients is concerned. It is really hard when the Lord won't let me raise any money or even talk about it. His words were, "When you need something come and talk to me. I will provide everything you need – the money, people, know how, and materials to get this job done."

Lord, show me how to be joyful even in my hour of discouragement. As I unlocked the door this morning I couldn't help thinking, "I will persevere even when it appears nothing is happening. Lord, let your beauty, love and holiness shine through me even when all looks lost." There were mornings when I unlocked the door at the beginning of the workday that I said, "Lord, I am here today, being faithful even if nothing happens." Make me content to trust your timing.

September 30, 1990

We did fairly well this first year of getting our bills paid and The Lord sent me the people that I needed and the money and the know-how. But now, one year after opening, I owed $1,000 of September rent and by the next day I would owe $1500 more. I was driving home from Louisville and told God, "Lord I've done everything you've asked me to do. I've been obedient, and you said you'd provide, and I owe $1,000 rent and tomorrow I'm going to owe him $2,500. The landlord is coming up from Florida next week and am going to have to talk to him face to face! How am I ever going to do that?! What am I supposed to say?!"

And God said, "Reova, do you remember the scripture that says to bring all your tithes into the storehouse and test me and prove me and see if I will not pour out on you a blessing greater than you're able to contain? I want you to go to the office tomorrow morning find out how much money is coming in September and write a check to another not-for- profit Christian organization in town for your tithe."

So on Monday morning I went, and I saw I needed to write a check for about $200 and I looked at the checkbook and I had $218, so I wrote the check and sent it off. That left less than $20 in the checking account. That meant while I owed $2500, I had just given away what little bit I had. I had no idea what would happen.

Thursday, I met with the landlord and was preparing to tell him I had no money for rent. I sat in a chair across from him and he started the conversation first. Before long, I noticed that this businessman who didn't seem to know a lot about God began to cry. Here he was pulling out tissues and wiping his eyes. Then he began to tell me he had a friend in town who was dying, and he knew this would be his last time to see him and it was weighing on him heavily. Then he said, "I'm a very different person than I was when you rented from me a year ago. I've been a horrible alcoholic, but I've been going to AA and I've been clean for 4 months." I sat quietly and he continued, "I've really been on a quest lately. You know I didn't grow up in a Christian home, but I have found the Lord and I'm hunting a church. Things are a lot different in my life now. I was bankrupt in almost every way when I met with you a year ago."

And then he said, "My quest for God began that afternoon in the parking lot when I first met you. I had been having a lot of trouble with vandalism in the building while I was an absent property owner. That day while I was working in the flowers, you pulled your car in and sat in that parking place for 3 hours and I got madder and madder. I said, 'Oh now I know where this vandalism is coming from!'"

"So", he said, "I left to go over to the Ramada Inn to get something to eat and I had too much to drink. When I came back and saw you were still there, I walked up to your car with the express purpose of telling you to get out of here and get your car off of my parking lot! But when I got over to your car, you were praying and I stood at your window listening to you pray. Tears were running down both of your faces, and I knew you had something that I didn't have. My quest for God began that afternoon in the parking lot. You will never know how many times after you closed at night, I would be back in here on the floor with my face on the carpet asking God to help me with the issues that I have in my life."

He continued to tell me more about what was going on in his life and I'd say, "Praise God, Praise God!", but all the time I'm thinking I needed to blurt out, "Dick, I owe you money! I have no money and you're not going to understand why I have no money, but we have to talk!"

Finally, after listening to him talk for about 45 minutes, I spoke up. "We have to talk money." And I began to tell the story simply and truthfully. When I had finished, he looked at me and said, "Reova, I don't understand faith, but I know you have a lot of it, and you can just pay me whenever you get the money."

My relief and surprise were matched only by the fact that during the six weeks he was in town we had enough money come in to pay September's rent, October's rent, and pay November's rent ahead of time! He just thought angels came and dumped the money on my desk, and as far as that's concerned, I did too! I thought, "I've finally won this battle! Surely The Lord has been testing me and I'll never have to worry about money again." I had the idea that when God said He would provide the money, that I would miraculously be able to sit down and write the rent check at the first of every month with no problem. Little did I know there would be bigger challenges coming than that $2500!

I was certain that The Lord would not let me raise funds and He wouldn't let me talk about it to anybody. He just said, "Come talk to me and I'll take care of it." But it didn't always seem like He was taking care of it. In my mind, He didn't take care of it, and He didn't take care of it, and He didn't take care of it, and at one point our rent bill got to $18,000 – an entire year's rent! Now, why Dick let me stay I don't know, but he did. And what I think is pretty exciting is that ever since the Lord provided the money to pay that $18,000, so far, that very first center has always had money in their bank account every month to pay more than their rent and utilities. I know it doesn't mean that is how it will always happen, but that's how it happened then.

Faith

"Faith isn't about what God does or doesn't do, it's about who God is and what he can do."

-Reova Meredith

Chapter Ten

FAITH

You will see in this chapter that Reova's struggle with money didn't end with just one lesson. Anyone who has ever started a business or a church or a ministry knows that money can be the single critical issue for failure or success and the single most stressful aspect. Perhaps that's why God uses money to teach us so many lessons. It's the one thing we feel like we can't live without and too much is not enough. The lessons that intertwine money with faith are many. They certainly can teach us what we believe about money and how we handle it. But perhaps the more important lessons are those that reveal our beliefs about faith, correct those beliefs, and grow our faith into something beautiful God uses to accomplish His purposes.

From Reova's Journal –

Tuesday, May 21, 1991

The Lord provided this promise from the life of Israel. Exodus 36:7, talking about the contribution for the tabernacle given to Moses, ...*because what they already had was more than enough to do all the work.* I have taken that as a promise that all financial consideration for the Center will be provided as needs arise. I held fast to the words of other saints, "What God orders, He pays for" and "If this is God's idea, I don't need money, I need faith."

My heart's cry through these years has been, "Lord, use this ministry to show the world what you will do in response to obedience and faith." I want the communities where we have local centers to know God is faithful and can be trusted without reservation.

Money came in trickles: six dollars was the amount left from someone's weekly grocery allowance, twenty-five dollars with a note, "Like the loaves and fishes, may this multiply."

In spite of tremendous displays of God's faithfulness, the biggest tests have come in area of finances. Tests in this area were so hard probably because we never had to depend on God to pay our household expenses. We were a two-income family and lived a frugal lifestyle, buying only that for which we knew we could pay.

Despite paying tithe, we are getting behind on rent again. The money just has not been coming in. I am paying tithe according to what has come in and paying what I can toward rent but it continues to build again.

I was driving home from visiting with my son's family thinking about the rent. I felt impressed to write our tithe check *in faith* for the amount we needed to come in, not for the amount that did come in. However, I had not spent enough time in prayer to 'try the spirit' so I only wrote the check for what had come in. The Lord wouldn't let me rest about this – to tithe on what we need. I decided when I got home, I would write a check for the difference, which I did.

June 3, 1991

The landlord called and needs money. I felt so faint-hearted. I now owe him $4000. "Lord, I don't understand this. I paid tithe on what we needed but very little came in. I certainly could use about $5000. I've been obedient and I'm testing you and proving you according to Malachi 3:10" The landlord needed our money right now, and I gave him all we had - $500.

I'm reading **Habakkuk 2:3,4**- *Though it linger, wait for it; it will certainly come and will not delay… But the righteous person will live by his faithfuness.* The Living Bible translation says, *Just be patient. They will not be overdue a single day.*

Isaiah 26:3- *He will keep in perfect peace all those who trust in him, whose thoughts turn often to the Lord!*

"Lord, I've been as obedient as I can be. I paid the tithe on what came in, then on what we needed – PLEASE, HELP!!!"

June 18, 91

I gave the landlord another $500. I still need $3000. "Help me to wait patiently for you to work this out. "

Thursday, June 27, 91

I'm really struggling over finances – "Lord, what am I do? Monday, I will owe $4500 in rent. When will this thing break? What is the answer to all this? I have been as obedient and faithful as I know how to be but there is no money coming in. Help me to be able to trust you even though I don't see what you're doing! I believe it was May 20th that I paid tithe on what we needed. Lord, that's five weeks ago and need has still not been provided. What am I to do? Show me all over again."

I wrote a reflection for the summer newsletter on waiting but I'm having trouble doing that. Please help me wait. Satan is tempting me to despair over this. "Lord, you have to help."

I've been searching scriptures again to remind me of God's provision. Here are some scriptures the Lord gave me midst the struggle with finances and my fear over the possible failure of the ministry:

Psalm 128:2 - *Blessings on all who reverence and trust the Lord—on all who obey him! Their reward shall be prosperity and happiness.*

Psalm 130:5- *I wait for the Lord, my whole being waits, and in his word I put my hope.*

Deuteronomy 28:1 If you fully obey the Lord your God…all these blessings will come on you…

> **v.8** *The Lord will send a blessing on everything you put your hand to.*
> **v.10** *Then all the peoples on earth will see that you are called by the name of the Lord.*
> **v. 11** *The Lord will grant you abundant prosperity.*
> **v. 12** *The Lord will bless all the work of your hands.*
> **v. 12b**- *You will lend to many nations but will borrow from none.*
> **v. 14**- *Do not turn aside from any of the commands I give you today.*

Sunday, July 7, 1991

I was able to give the landlord $1500. I still need $3000. "Lord, you know where that is."

Sunday, July 21, 1991

I was able to give the landlord $500. I still owe him $2500.

December 31, 1991

Someone gave me a check for $315 for the Center. I can give Dick some more on the $1105 I own him for December. "Lord, you know this money situation. It's so hard sometimes but help me to be able to trust you."

Later, I went to the mailbox. Someone sent a check for $1000. I finished the December rent and deposited $500 toward January rent. "Thank you, Lord, for supplying our needs. You are so good!"

I spent time in prayer reminding God I'm looking for 'big' things this next year, recommitting my life in obedience and service to Him. "Thank you, Lord for a powerful spirit filled 1991. I'm excited about 1992. You are going to do great things.

April 18, 1992

The end of March we received $2500 to be used anyway we pleased. A gal in my Bible Study who knew the donor said, "Getting $2500 from him is a miracle. He doesn't give to religious organizations."

September 14, 1992

I've been feeling we should not spend our energies to enter the Christmas Craft Fair at the mall this year. It brought us about $800 the last two years. I felt the Lord was telling me, "Reova, I sent you here to minister, not to raise funds. I told you I would provide what you need."

September 20, 1992

Many things are going well at the Center but I'm feeling the weight of no money to pay August and September rent. "Lord, should I have to beg you to pay your bills? I'm feeling like a fool for telling others I was obeying you. It feels like you are requiring a lot but leaving me to struggle through all this alone."

I was led to **II Chronicles 20:12-20-** *We have no power to face this vast army that is attacking us. We do not know what to do, but our eyes are on you... Do not be afraid or discouraged because of this vast army. For the battle is not yours, but God's... You will not have to fight this battle. Take up your positions; stand firm and see the deliverance the Lord will give you... and you will be successful."*

Thank you, Lord. I'm glad I've learned to turn to you when the way gets rough.

October 6, 1992

I calculated we owe $1105 for August rent, $1605 for September, and $1605 for October, for a total of $4315. "Lord, what is the answer? And you don't want me to do the craft fair? I know you will provide."

Faith has always been a great struggle in my life. Learning to trust God has not been an easy lesson. It seems that faith, as I had understood it, has not always worked in my life. And here's the question I have – Is there a place or a time in our Christian walk that we must have childlike faith… when we pray to God about things and believe that He will do them or give them to us? Then, does a time come as we mature and grow that God doesn't have to give us things or answer us immediately, but we still believe and love and trust Him anyway?

I think it is that childlike faith that believes the impossible will happen – that a miracle will take place. Then there are also times of unusual closeness with God when our prayers are answered in an obvious way and God seems especially intimate and caring.

C.S. Lewis believed that such striking answers to prayer typically come at the beginning of our walk with God. Then, as we proceed in our Christian life, these conspicuous answers tend to become more rare. [13]

The saying has been attributed to Thomas Aquinas that, "To one with faith, no explanation is necessary. But to one without faith, no explanation is possible."

Jesus often talked about the faith of a child. When a busy Mom goes about her day, she often buckles her child into the car seat and takes off on her errands. At the first stop, she takes the child by the hand and crosses busy streets and parking lots and heads into big intimidating buildings. It may be a grocery or a bank or a medical office. The child has no clue where they are going or what is happening inside the big building. They are only holding onto the hand of the one they trust completely without a care in the world. They don't fear or worry or scarcely even wonder. They just go along, being led by the one in charge. Similarly, faith never knows where it is being led, but it loves and knows the One who is leading. The root of faith is in knowing the person.

That all makes sense to us and sounds incredibly easy. But it rarely is that easy. We want control, we want a plan. We want our lives to run smoothly with no obstacles – or at least no obstacle we did not see ahead of time and plan for. But whose life is like that? No one's! That's why the life of faith can be so challenging. We refuse to sit back in our car seats and let God drive us wherever He needs us to go. Or, we have a hard time reconciling the things we are responsible for in this life with allowing Him to have complete control. Afterall, God isn't the one who completes our tax forms and signs the check and mails the envelope on time. There are things we can't just sit back and wait for Him to do. It would be ridiculous to think that way.

But that is exactly where our thinking about faith gets us in trouble. Faith means surrendering control of the circumstances we cannot control while acknowledging that somehow God is also always in control of the things we think we are in control of. He has ways of delaying the mail or hurrying up a check if He wants to. Our faith isn't about what God does or doesn't do, it's about who God is and what he *can* do.

Here are Reova's words on Faith –

> "Lord, you told me you wanted to use me to show the Christian community what you will do in response to obedience and faith. Obedience is no longer a struggle for me. I will be obedient when I know your will. However, faith is different. I continue to struggle with faith. Your Word says you will do what you promise, and you have. But sometimes I have had to wait for years in what felt like desperate situations. I know you have called me to show others faith and obedience but how do I do that when the struggle is so great? You have proven faithful, so why would I doubt? Yet still I seem to struggle with uncertainty and doubt."

"I have cried, screamed, repented, obeyed, and tried to understand your ways, yet sometimes my emotions and feelings and talk have been stronger than my exercise of faith. It's like a train of fact, faith and feelings and sometimes I think my feelings have been pulling that train. Help me move forward on fact – on the fact that your Word says you will do exactly what you say you will do. I know I can trust your Word by faith. My feelings are not reliable. They are not fact or faith."

In her now dated book, *Meal in a Barrel*, Amy Carmichael, the missionary to India, said, "Faith has nothing to do with circumstances. It deals entirely with the Word of God. Faith does not feed upon the experiences of others. Its food is found in the promises of God."

Someone once said that faith is acting as if God were telling the truth. Faith means we are taking God at His word. We trust God for who He is and not because things always equal out or make sense, or because we have satisfying answers to our questions and petitions. Faith may *want* answers but is able to survive without them.

When the Lord called me to found the Center For Women's Ministries (CWM), I felt I was leaving the ease of my church where things were comfortable, for the uncertainty of uncharted places. Leaving the carpenter shop is never easy. And God doesn't show us the whole road ahead. He only gives us one step at a time.

We are all familiar with the testing of our faith. My faith has been tested many times. One memorable testing stands out as a great lesson for me… because I failed the same test miserably nine years earlier.

At that time, my family was headed to Brazil in South America to build a church in my deceased husband's memory. Our trip was looming and two of our visas had not yet arrived. The Lord sent me to Genesis 22:8 and 14, where three times the promise was given:

God Himself will provide.
The Lord will provide.
It will be provided.

The Lord said, "Don't do anything about this. I will provide." Now within days of departure, even though I knew God was saying, "Trust me", I made a call to see if the visas had arrived. They had not. But my sons were able to pick them up at 9:30 the morning of our 11:30 am flight.

Nine years later, my family was headed back to Brazil, and for a month I was tested about the visas to see if I would obey and whether my faith had grown. Five passports were still missing, and I was so tempted numerous times to check on their arrival. I even put off talking to my kids at all for fear I would ask about the passports. As I struggled to trust that God would do what He said He would do, He again sent me back to Genesis 22, as well as to the following scriptures:

II Chronicles 20:17 – *You will not have to fight this battle. Stand firm and see the deliverance the Lord will give you.*

V 20 – *Have faith in the Lord and you will be successful.*

Psalm 5:3 – *I lay my requests before you and wait expectantly.*

Romans 4:20-21 – *Yet he did not waver through unbelief regarding the promise of God, but was strengthened in his faith and gave glory to God, being fully persuaded that God had power to do what he had promised.*

Psalm 34:4,6 – *I sought the Lord, and he answered me; he delivered me from all my fears. This poor man called, and the Lord heard him and saved him out of all his troubles.*

Romans 9:16 – *It does not, therefore, depend upon human desire or effort, but on God's mercy.*

Throughout the time leading up to our trip, my family called several times, but I did not ask about the passports. I prayed continually but was obedient to trust God. Finally, not long before departure, I got the call telling me that all passports and visas had arrived. Praise God! He is faithful!

From that experience, I learned the following lessons:

1. If you fail the test of obedience, God will bring a similar situation later to give you another opportunity to obey. (Maybe nine years later!)

2. From **Mark 11:23** – *if anyone does not doubt in their heart but believes that what they say will happen, it will be done for them* .Rather than the struggles of belief being in my heart, they were in my head (my mind). Satan attacks the mind, and the struggle I was having with belief in these and many other situations was from Satan. So I began to take thoughts captive and make them obedient to Christ according to II Corinthians 10:5.

3. God can be trusted to do exactly what He says He will do. His will, His way, His timing!

Aside from the lessons I learned from the visa testing, I have since come to realize there seem to be several general and common tests of Faith. In my observation, experience, and study, I have separated them into 3 categories. There's the **faith to risk**, the **faith to trust**, and the **faith to surrender**. The test of **faith to risk** is a command to leave the known and go into the unknown; to leave a comfort zone for an uncomfortable zone. Jesus left the comforts of home and the carpenter shop for a new and active life.

While all these tests have a common denominator of fear, no test is more affected by fear than the **faith to risk**. The American

Association of Christian Counselors provides its members with a professional journal. Author Ken Nichols shares a story that beautifully illustrates the fear and **faith to risk** connection. He tells the story of a young family whose house caught fire one night, leaving their young son on the roof of the burning home. The father was below begging his son to jump to him, but the smoke, flames and darkness prevented the boy from being able to see his father. Finally, the terrified boy screamed, "But Daddy, I can't see you!" The wise father hollered back up, "It's OK, son, I can see you, and that's all that matters! Just jump and I will catch you!" The boy jumped safely into his father's arms. The **faith to risk** requires jumping despite our fears.

Then there's the test of **faith to trust**. When the Lord asks us to step out in obedience, He promises to provide what we need to do what He has asked us to do. Someone once told me, "What God orders, He pays for." He promised me if I would establish CWM He would provide the money, the know-how, the people and the materials to successfully accomplish His bidding. Many times, His timing was not my timing. I have been tested repeatedly on God's faithfulness where timing was concerned. But look how long Abraham and Caleb each had to wait before God's promises to them became reality. His ways are not our ways.

Finally, there's the test of **faith to surrender**. God expects explicit obedience. He often asks us to sacrifice the thing most precious to us. We all have our "Isaacs". For me, it was ambition. I wanted to become a college professor, and I waited ten long years for the offer to come and the dream to knock on my door. But when it came, the Lord said, "I have taught you too much about living the Christian life for you to spend the rest of your life teaching teachers how to teach."

Soon after that I wrote in my journal; "Jesus, I my cross have taken. I've left all to follow thee. Gone is the ambition to do great things, pride of accomplishments and abilities, security of job, insurance and retirement. Tonight, Lord, I stand naked before you with nothing to give but my availability to be used by you. Come, Lord, and take the brokenness of my life, the emptiness of myself and let it spring forth in fruitfulness for you."

When my surrender of that dream and ambition was complete, His plan for CWM began to unfold. I have found God's plan is always best. I now believe that before faith can take hold, all selfish desires have to be put to death. We can want only what will bring glory to God. We can't want something because it will reduce our pain – even the salvation of a spouse, or because it will reduce our losses – even life and death situations of a child we love, or because it increases our comforts- like a new home or car, or because it feeds our pride, like a promotion at work. Our *only* motive must be whatever brings glory to God!

This idea of faith has greatly affected my life of trusting God. It's easy to say that I believe God can do something or that I believe God will supply all my needs, but when those tests come, to prove that I believe is often another story. I have been tested so many times over the past years I can't count them. But I know that faith *must* be tested because it can only become personal through conflict or difficulty. "Lord, please help me to show others you can be trusted… that you will do exactly what you say you will do!"

Chapter Eleven

A WORD ABOUT WAITING – THE HARDEST PART OF FAITH

June 28, 1991

This reflection that I wrote for the summer newsletter pretty well sums up the struggle I have with waiting. I've received several responses about how much this helped those who read it.

That shows me how difficult this lesson on waiting is for most of us.

> One of the hardest things the Lord has asked me to do is 'WAIT". I find scriptures marked throughout my Bible instructing me to 'wait on the Lord'. The one marked with the most dates beside it is **Psalm 27:14**- *Wait on the Lord, be strong and take heart and wait for the Lord.* This scripture has six dates written beside it, which I do when the Lord speaks to me through a specific scripture, I write the date beside it and often the situation to which it is speaking in my life.

> Waiting is the hardest work I do. I've often cried with the **Psalmist,** *My eyes are straining to see your promises come true. When will you comfort me with your help? I am*

exhausted with waiting... But still I cling to your laws and obey them. How long must I wait? Psalm 119:82-84 TLB

Philip Brooks, a New England preacher, known for his outward calmness and poise, was one day pacing the floor like a caged lion. When asked, "What is the trouble?" replied, "I'm in a hurry but God isn't." Haven't you felt that way sometimes? I have.

Pastor Earl Lee, whose son was hostage in the Iraq crisis said, "It is not God's answers that are hard to accept, it's His timing." As I've waited for God to provide for the financial needs here at the Center, sometimes I'm tempted to cry "Lord, how long must I wait for you to do what you promised?" The answer comes back, *If it seems slow, do not despair for these things will surely come to pass. Just be patient. They will not be overdue a single day* Habakkuk 2:3TLB.

Theologian Andrew Murray declared, "Be assured that if God waits longer than you wish, it only makes the blessing doubly precious. God will not delay one hour too long."

Sixteen years ago while I was applying for various administrative positions in the school system, the Lord gave me **Psalm 18:43**- *People I did not know are subject to me.* I thought that was a promise I would receive one of those promotions. I did not. Fourteen years later, as we opened the Center, with me as director, the Lord pointed back to that forgotten promise and said, "I now have you ready for leadership." The Lord had been pruning my life from self-sufficiency, pride, feelings of success and wrong focus. It took the Lord fourteen more years to prepare me to guide others. Sometimes we wait because we are not ready nor prepared for the answer.

John Newton, the redeemed slave master said, "The Lord's time is like the time of the tide which no human presence can either accelerate or retard. Though it tarry, WAIT for it".

LORD, HELP US WAIT.

There is the familiar saying, "Practice makes perfect." Any skill attempted will never be perfected without *doing* it... over and over. That includes the skill of waiting. Reova had asked God to help her wait. People say not to ask for patience because God will put something in your life to help you develop patience. The same may be said for waiting. The question here is, does waiting build faith, or is faith required to wait? Maybe a little of both are accurate.

More from Reova's Faith Devotions-

> Theologian Peter Kreeft has said, "The answer to suffering is not an answer at all. It's the Answerer. It's Jesus Himself. It's a person! THE person!" Jesus is more than an explanation. He's what we really need. The ultimate answer is Jesus' presence!
>
> One of the books I refer to often that has helped me immensely with the idea of waiting for God to answer prayers is by Bob Sorge. In his book, *The Fire of Delayed Answers, Sorge says,* "Sometimes God delays the answers to our prayer in order to produce a greater maturity and fruitfulness in us. God's first priority in our lives is to make us fruitful – not to make us comfortable."
>
> Sorge says the three things that delayed answers bring are:
>
> 1. A purified faith
> 2. A kindling of our love to new depths of passion and maturity
> 3. A further developing of Christlikeness in our lives

Isaiah 64:4 in The Message says, *A God like you works for those who wait for Him.*

We recall that God had Abraham and Sarah wait for what was promised to them. Finally, when all hope was exhausted, God provided supernaturally. Jesus also waited 30 years to begin a three-year ministry. His Father had Him wait and prepare 10 years for every year of ministry He would eventually have. The Lord wants to bring you to a clearer understanding of finding your strength in quietness and confidence. When it seems that the Lord isn't listening to us, it's a sure sign that we are on the edge of a new level of depth in our relationship with our Lord.

It is difficult to understand how or why waiting for God to answer our prayers at times is such a vital part of faith. When you think about it, much of our prayer life is devoted to requests. "Help me through this situation, heal me, heal somebody else, grant wisdom or favor, change hearts, provide finances, change circumstances", and the list can go on and on. We are constantly asking for whatever will make our lives easier or less painful. And for sure, God wants us to do that. He has asked us to bring all our burdens to Him, promising His yoke is easy. Philippians 4:6 encourages us to let our requests be made known to God. But it can be rather myopic at the same time. Most of our prayers are centered around whatever benefits us. And most of the time, we don't hesitate to tell God exactly how we think He should work it out. We are all about answers to our prayers, and the sooner the better!

In his famous devotional, Oswald Chambers says about prayer, "We are not to insist on answers from God when we pray but the motive should be to get ahold of God, not answers." The sincere question for our faith then is, how is God enough when we are still suffering, or still in desperate need, and the answers we prayed for do not come?

It may help us to affirm that our faith is not about what God does or does not do for us. We *think* our faith is strengthened when God answers our prayers, and the earth moves, and miraculously, all is well. And indeed, that is a wonderful thing. But it is often quickly forgotten as soon as the next crisis comes. When His answer is Yes, it's amazing, and even if He answers No, we eventually accept it. But when the answer is neither Yes nor No, but Wait... that is often the hardest. Our faith cannot be about what God does or does not do for us, rather it must be about God's *character*. It is about *who* He is and what He *can* do. We must learn to leave the how and the when totally up to Him.

Our faith is made stronger in the waiting when we acknowledge that His character is loving toward us and working for our good. Our faith is made stronger in the waiting when we acknowledge that His character is Sovereign and that He alone sees the end from the beginning, and He alone knows what is best for His children whom He loves so much. Our faith is made stronger in the waiting when we acknowledge that His character is patient. While for us, it feels as though time is running out for whatever request we are desperate for, time never runs out for God Almighty. He owns all of time and eternity and is never, ever in a hurry. In his book, *Fire of Delayed Answers,* Bob Sorge' writes, "We're impatient because we have limited resources. God has unlimited resources so He can wait as long as he wants! God longs to reveal His ways to men, but they can be made known only to those who will agree to wait."

Finally, our faith is made stronger in the waiting when we acknowledge that His character neither slumbers nor sleeps and that His plans and purposes will always be accomplished and nothing on earth or in the heavens can thwart His plans. What He purposes continually marches on, always unfolding exactly as He intends. He is working. He is not slacking or ignoring. He sees all and knows all. His ways are perfect, and He is trustworthy!

When we acknowledge those truths about God and about His character, we can stand on those truths. We can walk in certainty because of who our God is and what our God can do. We walk in certainty knowing His love for us is extravagant and protective. We walk by faith in the waiting, and our faith is strengthened. No one would think that an overly indulged child who is never told No and is immediately given his every request would grow into a mature adult, strong in conviction, wise in decision-making, and reliable in difficulty. Why would we see ourselves any differently with our Heavenly Father?

Chapter Twelve

WALKING THE WALK OF FAITH

With the first Center up and running, so much of the work was in the past. Sacrifices made, surrender accomplished, and obedience pursued at every turn. The new dream had finally been realized, and it was now time to sit back and enjoy the fruits of all the hard work. Never! Where God has a plan and gives a vision, Satan will always jump in and wreak havoc to try and prevent good from happening.

Only God knew the future of His plan for CWM but throughout the next few years, His plans for growth and for the scope of counseling and training would slowly be revealed. Those plans were not without challenges, of course. And Reova would not only have to lean heavily on the lessons God had been teaching her, but she would need to teach those same lessons to the volunteers who were now such an important part of the ministry. In her words...

Summer 1991

The ministry here at the Center has at least doubled in volume since our first-year anniversary last October. Also, the magnitude of spiritual needs we are dealing with requires intensified wisdom and spiritual discernment.

During this past year, and especially the last three months, God has been powerfully working in the lives of the volunteers. In prayer about a month ago I expressed these thoughts, "Lord, I feel the volunteers are growing so much that they are just dragging me along. How can I lead when they are becoming so powerful in you?"

The Lord answered back, "You have to spend more time with me in prayer and the WORD if you are going to lead this ministry as it grows and develops in spiritual depth and increased quantity."

In sharing with the Tuesday morning intercessory group what God had shown me, I asked them to pray that He would reveal how to do that with my already busy schedule.

As we prayed the Lord disclosed to me a plan: "Move your office to the lower level so you are away from the exciting activities (which I love). Double the volunteer staff – have one person covering the reception area and phone, and another available as a counseling volunteer. The counseling volunteer can cover scheduled appointments as well as be available for 'walk-ins'. Doing this frees you from most of the client load. Transform your office into a volunteer office and work room."

In less than a week the plan was being implemented. My office has been moved, the volunteer office has been furnished with new donated furniture and presently we are filling the 'double' volunteer schedule.

All of this reminds me that where God guides, He will provide. I continue to say, "Thank You, Lord, for making me worthy, then choosing me to lead this exciting, vibrant, outreaching ministry for women who desire to know you better. Continue to teach me so I can teach others."

August, 1991

I've been doing a study of the development of faith by trial, from James 1:3, which produces endurance, steadfastness, and patience. I have come to realize in a new way that what God is desiring to develop in me, is a relationship. The giving of the desires of my heart, my wishes, are an outgrowth of the relationship. He could give me everything I want in a minute, but that would not develop the relationship. Lord, make me to continuously desire the relationship, the giver, not the gifts. Help me to want you more than anything I desire personally or that I want for ministry development.

August 16-17

Over the past several months, God has been teaching me new lessons on prayer and obedience. He has been very convincing that my personal life and ministry effectiveness here at the Center are requiring more time in prayer.

Recently, I spent a two-day solitary prayer and fasting retreat at a lake condo. The personal benefits were so powerful.

Loaded with my Bible, spiritual journal, sealed prayer requests from volunteers, praise tapes, two bags filled with study books, commentaries, uncompleted work, pads of writing paper, fruit juice, and a few personal items, I packed the car. Before I left the driveway, God was very present, assuring me this would be an experience to change my life.

I literally spent 30 hours "on the mountain" with Jesus. I had expected to write a retreat presentation that I was to give in a few weeks, to read the books I'd brought along, to plan and schedule. But God designed my days much more effectively than those preconceived plans. All I really needed to take was my Bible, journal, praise tapes and the sealed prayer requests.

I discovered during those hours the necessity of varying spiritual activity. Intercessory prayer is physically and emotionally difficult work. It needs to be couched in times of praise, reading scripture and meditation. The praise tapes were playing almost constantly throughout the two days. They seemed to set the tone for whole personal retreat.

I'm anxious to repeat this experience regularly. I know now prayer does not *precede* the battle. Prayer *is* the battle. Victory and success in our daily lives, in ministry, and in relationships, are fought and won in prayer. My challenge is to spend more energy in communion with God.

Fall, 1991

Girls began to come into the center for help with sexual abuse issues and issues they had from being in the occult. These were not things I was prepared to handle. I had expected us to minister to women who had marital issues, or grief issues. While marital and grief issues are not easy either, I felt more prepared in how to help in those circumstances. Sexual abuse was just now beginning to be talked about publicly. Churches were not prepared to deal with this issue and certainly not the occult or satanic oppression and possession.

When these girls came, I asked the Lord to not 'make me do this'. But that did not seem to be God's plan. One girl I counseled with for the next few years was in leadership in the local coven. During the months I worked with her, she was still in contact with the coven. She was taking information back and forth between me and the members of the local coven.

During this time, I was scared. They knew where I lived. They would appear at the Center's parking lot. They told her they had a 'hit list' of 14 names which they were out to destroy. She told them, "You won't be able to touch her, there is too much of the spirit of God upon her." They responded, "We know that, but we sure would like to try."

The Lord sent me to Psalm 91:11 AMPC *He will give His angels especial charge over you to accompany and defend and preserve you in all your ways [of obedience and service.]* I felt The Lord saying, "As long as you are doing this in obedience to me, I will protect you and nothing hurtful will come from your interaction with these clients."

The Lord then sent me to Psalm 91:13 *You will tread on the lion and cobra; You will trample the great lion and the serpent .* His personal interpretation to me was, "Remember the wizard in the "Wizard of Oz", how he bellowed and frightened everyone who came near but when they pulled the curtain, he was a little, dried-up character that was shivering in his boots, scared to death? That is Satan is in the face of my power. He bellows but is frightened to death of my power in you." I knew that Satan was not one bit afraid of Reova, but he is mightily afraid of God's power in me!

That Psalm goes on in v.14-16, *Because he loves me," says the Lord, "I will rescue him; I will protect him, for he acknowledges my name. He will call on me, and I will answer him; I will be with him in trouble, I will deliver him and honor him.With long life I will satisfy him and show him my salvation."*

Mid-January, 1992

A gal came into the Center and told me how the occult has "Christian Counselors" planted to take the messages back to the occult. She said, "They are getting hot on your trail." When she began to talk about how careful I should be, I pointed out how God had promised His protection and shared with her about the lion in Wizard of Oz.

When I asked her if she would like us to pray together before she left, she said No. I was left with a lot of oppression and very mixed feelings about the meeting. Did she really want help? Was she planted to make us fearful to proceed? Or was she just trying to find out what we are doing?

At one point in our discussion, I asked her if all ritual, occult practices were perverted sex. She said, "Yes. When they sexually abuse you, they rape your body. When they abuse you ritualistically, they rape your soul." These are especially spiritual and emotional implications.

I left the Center still troubled over the afternoon. On the way home the Lord met with me and promised His protection. I was weeping asking for wisdom, a covering, and praising Him for making us worthy, and for being a friend. This scripture came to me again, Jeremiah 1:8, *Do not be afraid of them for I am with you and will rescue you.*

When I got home this evening, this message was on our answering machine. "I know who you are and what you are doing." TRUST!

July 16, 1992

I've been on a real emotional drain the last few days. Yesterday about 4:15 I got a call from the Bloomington Workforce wanting to know what kind of landlord Dick was. She said," I'm a friend of someone you know, and we are going to be renting the other side of the building. We're to get the lease next week."

My friend walked in five minutes after I hung up the phone. She said, "That's the organization I worked for when it was named The Occupational Developmental Center. It has a new name now. Anyone applying for welfare has to go through there; ex-cons, mental patients going back into society and anyone who may be at-risk for a stable living."

I simply went into a frenzy. I went over and anointed the building claiming it for the Center for Women's Ministries. I went to my office and pleaded with God. I pulled out all the scriptures the Lord had given me a few months before when I was dealing with a lot of uncertainty.

I kept thinking surely this was a trick of Satan. If those offices move in here, we will no longer be safe here. Our ministry will simply be destroyed. The women are so fragile anyway.

I called the landlord and asked him what he understood the tenants to be like next door. He understood they are an office operation, needing five parking spaces, spending all day on computers. I told him what I had been told about the potential tenants and my concern for our physical and emotional safety.

He replied, "I told you I wouldn't allow anything on the property not compatible with what you're doing. I'll check into this and get back to you."

July 18, 1992

The landlord called back and had done some checking about the tenants going in next door. From his search he says they are only an administrative office operation and do not deal with the clients. "Thank you, Lord, you still care!"

August 5,1992

I am really struggling personally. We did not get the building we wanted. The grant I felt we should ask for did not come through. A couple of new ministries that have come to town are ministries that I have encouraged and supported. While they seem to be taking off, I feel I am going in reverse at the Center.

I feel rather foolish, like I really can't distinguish your voice. And while I know your credibility is not at stake, my credibility at being able to hear your voice is very much in jeopardy. Down deep I still believe you have spoken to me, and I haven't been mistaken, but right now everything looks really black. I feel like I'm in a dark night of the soul. This has been going on for about a month.

Lord, I don't want to be jealous of someone else's success in ministry. Help me know how to let go and let you. Right now I feel you are requiring more and more from me, but I am getting more hurt and heartache and disappointment.

What more of me is there to relinquish, give up, or turn loose of that I haven't already given up? I know you're in control. You're working all things for my good and your glory. I know your ways are higher than mine. I know you are refining me, but this process hurts so much when I've done everything I know to do to be obedient to you.

I'm not looking for a reward in Heaven. I just want to be obedient to you. I just want a close relationship with you, but it seems the cost is so high. I've told you I'll pay the price. Help me to never change my mind. I feel like I've given up all of 'self' but you seem to keep finding more areas of my life that need crucified. This process hurts and I don't like it. It feels like I experience victory for a season, then I'm down in the pit again. Lord, I want to get to the place in my relationship with you that loss and gain are all the same as long as I'm in the center of your will.

Hope

"*What is Hope? Hope is the assurance of the faithfulness of God.*"

-REOVA MEREDITH

Chapter Thirteen

GROWTH AND FURTHER DEVELOPMENT – HOPE REALIZED

The next several years brought exponential growth and development, along with exponential challenges – some new and some more of the same. To be sure, where God intends to go, Satan will throw obstacles at every turn. God's plans for CWM, however, would never be thwarted, just as His plans and purposes for His children, organizations, churches, governments, and nations. Isaiah 14:26-27 reminds us, *This is the plan determined for the whole world; this is the hand stretched out over all nations. For the Lord Almighty has purposed, and who can thwart Him? His hand is stretched out, and who can turn it back?*

Reova continued to listen closely to God's instructions to stay true to the foundational directives He had given her years before. Every new center was established with the same procedure beginning with a season of prayer between several committed women who would form the advisory committee. God would provide the Center director and the space for the new center in His time. New centers were being requested across the Midwest as word spread of this much needed free counseling for women by trained volunteers. It was more than evident God saw the need long before He called Reova, and the growth explosion was the barometer for how great the need was.

Just as new centers were being established, the organization was being solidified with policies and procedures, board members, grant-writing, and vision-casting for what the future of CWM may look like. Reova may have felt inadequate for the task amidst so much change and growth, but like Romans 11:29, she was certain her *calling was irrevocable*. She would continue to do all she knew to do – lean in, listen, and obey.

In her leaning in, God was teaching her more about intimacy with Him being the real goal – not just more centers or in-the-black balance sheets. In her listening, He was beginning to reveal exactly how He would use CWM to heal more and more women's hearts so they, too could learn about intimacy with Him. And in her obeying, God was giving her new experiences to trust Him with. She had inklings all along of this ministry being far-reaching, but in the next few years, God would begin to put into motion His plans, turning her inklings into desires and her desires into hopes. Eventually, those hopes would become reality.

Before the ministry would be trusted with so many hopes for the future, God intended that Reova would learn more and more about Hope. Hope for the ministry and for her life was not only to be about plans and visions and desires. Hope was to be found in this more intimate relationship with Him and His Word. And she would learn that Hope is always born out of struggle.

Here are Reova's words on Hope –

Hope – The Worst Thing to be Without

Someone once noted, "Man can live 40 days without food, 3 days without water, and 8 minutes without air, but only 1 second without hope.

From *The Sacred Romance,* author John Eldridge says, "Our hearts cannot live without hope. Gabriel Marcel says that 'hope is for the soul what breathing is for the living organism.' In the trinity of Christian graces – faith, hope, and love – love may be the greatest, but hope plays the deciding role. Faith and love depend on hope, our anticipation of what lies ahead: Faith and love . . . spring from the hope that is stored up for you in heaven" (Col. 1:5)

During the WWII bombings, stories have been told of the thousands of orphans who were left starving. The fortunate were rescued and placed in refugee camps. But because of the extent of stress and loss in their lives, they often couldn't sleep at night. They feared waking up to being homeless and starving. When nothing comforted them, the caretakers decided to give them a piece of bread to hold on to at bedtime. By holding on to their bread, these children could sleep in peace. All through the night the bread reassured them, "Today I ate, and I will eat again tomorrow" – that's what hope will do.

In the classic allegory from 1678 titled *The Pilgrim's Progress*, author and Puritan preacher John Bunyan tells the story about Christian and his companion, Hopeful, who are on their way to heaven. By mistake they take the wrong road (Bypath Meadow) and end up in Doubting Castle being tortured by Giant Despair. Finally, when near death, Christian remembers that he has a key, given to him earlier on his journey, that can open any door. That key is called "Promise". With the promises of God, he and Hopeful escape the dungeon and get back on the King's Highway.

True hope is the reliance on the promises of Jesus, expecting the promises to be fulfilled. In spite of situations that seem utterly hopeless, we can still say, "God will provide a way. His Word promises!" JESUS IS HOPE. His Word is full of these promises.

Proverbs 23:18- *There is surely a future hope for you and your hope will not be cut off.*
Psalm 119:114- *I have put my hope in your word.*
Jeremiah 29:11- *[My plans are to] give you a hope and a future.*
Hebrews 10:23- *Let us hold unswervingly to the hope we profess, for He who promised is faithful.*

Psalm 33:20-*We wait in hope for the Lord, He is our help and our shield.*
Psalm 42:11- *Put your hope in God, for I will yet praise Him, my Savior and my God.*

The Day I Began to Understand Hope:

It was in January of 2003 when my good friend and long-time supporter of the ministry lost her son to an accidental overdose. My friend had prayed hours and years for this child, often meeting with others to pray, myself included.

This young boy had given his life to Christ, but like many teens, his behavior did not always exhibit what we believe life in Christ is all about.

We are clear that only God knows our hearts, but still, there was heart-wrenching confusion and fear about his eternal soul. Personally, my dilemma with his death was what to do with scriptures such as Acts 16:31 that says, *Believe in the Lord Jesus, and you will be saved—you and your household."* Or Matthew 18:19 that says, *Again, truly I tell you that if two of you on earth agree about anything they ask for, it will be done for them by my Father in heaven.* Salvation of a soul is God's desire – He died for it.

Or, what about Psalm 37:4? *Delight yourself in the Lord and He will give you the desires of your heart.* Surely the desire of every mother's heart is for her children to be in heaven.

During this time, my friend was led to these scriptures; Proverbs 3:5- 6- *Trust in the Lord with all your heart and lean not on your own understanding.* She had to admit, "Lord, I don't understand." But the word came back in her spirit, "You are not supposed to understand - only trust."

Then she was led to Psalm 56:3- *When I am afraid, I will trust in you.* Again she had to confess, "I am afraid, Lord." Reading on to verse 4, with courage she claimed, *In God I trust, I will not be afraid.* Her courage and trust was affirmed with John 14:1 *Do not let your hearts be troubled. Trust in God, trust also in me.* She wrote these words on paper memorizing the promises and truths and carried them with her for a long time. Anytime she was overwhelmed, she read those scriptures, or even just reached in to touch them, sometimes many times a day, and took courage.

As the days wore on, my dear grieving friend received these scriptures; Psalm 106:43-45, *Many times he delivered them but they were bent on rebellion and wasted away in their sin. But he took note of their distress when he heard their cry, for their sake he remembered his covenant and out of his great love he relented.* And John 14:13-14 - *And I will do whatever you ask in my name, so that the son may bring glory to the Father. You may ask me for anything in my name and I will do it.*

Because of God's promises and her obedience in prayer, my friend was finding HOPE! One day she said, "It doesn't make sense that I have hope, but I do because of Christ and what He said." She trusted in God because of His Word! She now trusts that her son has eternal life because God, in His mercy, is faithful to His promises - His promise to accept that her son had believed on the Lord Jesus Christ and was saved. Hope is found in Jesus as revealed by the scriptures.

Two years later, she shared the scripture in John 13:1-17 where Jesus is washing the disciples' feet before being betrayed. Verse 7 jumped out as a promise to both of us! *You do not realize now what I'm doing but later you will understand.* And God says it again in Jeremiah 23:20 - *In days to come you will understand it clearly.*

I'm seeing more clearly that HOPE is wrapped up and dependent upon accepting the promises of God - the scriptures, not our circumstances. It is not dependent on whether we understand or don't understand, but whether we wholly trust and accept His

Word as Truth. If God's Word cannot be trusted, if the Bible is not the inspired Word of God, there is no hope on earth.

In her classic book, *Edges of His Ways,* author Amy Carmichael further explains, "We cannot fill ourselves with Hope, for we have no wells of hope within us, but God has. Just as He is the God of Love, He is the God of Hope and we can pray, 'Hope through me, Hope of God.'"

Hope is born when, in the midst of hopeless circumstances, we trust and accept what God says in His Word. As we put our trust in Him (because of what He has promised in is Word), His Hope grows in us as He begins to work changing us. Hope rises in our hearts when we see God using the pressures of our circumstances to conform us to the image of Christ – to make us more like Jesus.

Hebrews 7:18 says, *A better hope, Jesus Christ, is introduced, by which we draw near to God.* Jesus is Hope! He is a better Hope than we might conjure up ourselves. Hope is rooted in our relationship with Christ Himself. Hope is what He has promised. Hope is our natural response when we see the character of Jesus developing in our lives! That is not always easy. It is born out of struggle, out of hopeless circumstances that cause us to question and require us to trust. Hope will not grow if we are committed only to our comfort. Suffering and loss and grief and struggle are a part of this life. In the midst of these, we wrestle with God, eventually finding comfort as we accept His promises and that births hope. That hope grows as we submit to His Hand that lovingly molds us, in the midst of our suffering and struggle, to be more like Him.

Hope can be a painful process. While waiting in hope, the process is often filled with sorrow, pain, and disappointment. Because the path toward hope is one of suffering, sorrow and pain. In my Bible next to Psalm 22:1 where David says, *My God, My God why have you forsaken me?,* I have these words written, "Spoken on the cross when total aloneness and full acceptance touched each other – when God's absence was most expressed, God's presence was profoundly revealed. We encounter HOPE at the intersection of absence and presence."

Hope begins when the memory of what we have lost (absence) is replaced with a longing for what is to be restored (presence.) We must grieve these losses before hope comes, whether that is a marriage, a job, a lost one, or anything else. Hope is always life-giving.

Choosing to respond to hope requires courage, vision, and patience. Our hope begins with the fact that we know He LOVES us.

What is Hope? Hope is the assurance of the faithfulness of God.

Chapter Fourteen

HOPE GROWS... TO THE UTTERMOST PARTS OF THE EARTH!

The lessons God had been teaching Reova on Love, Prayer, Obedience, Faith, and Hope were put to the test many times since God first gave her the assignment to help hurting women. They had been put to the test, and the blessings, rewards, and struggles had accompanied each lesson. While God was honing each concept deep in her soul – in her personal relationship with Him, He was also using the ministry as right-in-front-of -your-eyes object lessons! Every single thing God was teaching her was being cemented in her heart as it played out right before her in the ministry.

There was still another aspect of Hope God had been waiting to reveal to Reova. It is found in Romans 8:24-25. *But hope that is seen is no hope at all. Who hopes for what they already have? But if we hope for what we do not yet have, we wait for it patiently.*

Reova's journals tell the story of Hope blossoming and growing. In her words -

May 16, 1994

Here are some scriptures that came to me this morning -

2 Samuel 22:44 CEB - *You appointed me the leader of many nations.*
Psalm 18:43 CEB repeats it - *You appointed me the leader of many nations.*

The Lord first gave me these scriptures 14 years ago. At that time I thought it meant I would get a principalship in the school system. Now this morning it feels like it is being fulfilled by the Center coming into being. Are these scriptures confirmation that the Center for Women's Ministries will spread around the world? Psalm 18:49 says, *I will praise you among the nations, O Lord, I will sing to your name!*

Today I found this in my journal from December 1991. I had this conversation with Dick, the Landlord, about our first building on Gourley Pike. He said this, "Those of us in AA have a hallowed spot in Akron, Ohio, the home of the man who began AA. It's thought of as sort of a shrine, like the beginning place of a mighty healing organization. Reova, I believe someday this building you are in will be sort of a shrine – the beginning of an organization that will spread across the nation."

I said, "Dick, that's how I feel! That is my vision, but it's so neat for you to be able to see that happening too." Thank you, Lord for that confirmation of what's ahead.

February 1997

At this point in 1997 we have six centers open! I thought the Lord was going to ask me to open up ONE center for women's ministries and then eventually I was just going to retire... really retire! But other communities began to call us. They all said, "Our community needs what you have. Can you help us?"

Now when they approach us about coming into their community, we help them by giving them instructions and providing materials so they can gather their people within their own community. Each community is responsible for their own building, their own volunteers, and their own finances. We provide oversight and help them get started. It has been amazing to me how the communities have evolved. We're in several states at this time and growing.

Still, I feel the Lord continues to give me scriptures as a promise of growing even further - world-wide.

Genesis 22:18 - *All nations on earth will be blessed because you have obeyed me.*
Colossians 1:6 - *All over the world the gospel is bearing fruit and growing as it has been doing among you.*
Psalm 1:8- *I will make the nations your inheritance.*
Ps. 9:11- *Proclaim among the nations what He has done.*

April 16, 1998

This evening I've been watching a Billy Graham special on T.V. They showed scenes from his 1960 and 1973 African tours. I just have this flutter inside of me of the day the Center for Women's Ministries will be there. I hope I get to go before I die.

Sunday, February 21,1999

This evening I've been reflecting on how I am going to get to do what I feel God has shown me will happen. I believe I'm to spread these centers around the world and I'm to tell the world God can be trusted and He is faithful to His promises. He will do what He said He would do in response to prayer.

As I've reflected, I don't see how that can happen. I've had only limited exposure over the last years. I feel what I have to say is powerful but is it powerful enough for the world to want to hear it?

I've read, "Ministry comes without promotion to the ready and waiting heart!" Lord, am I ready? I am waiting! If I'm not ready, get me ready.

Isaiah 41:9 *I took you from the ends of the earth, from its farthest corners I called you. I said, you are my servant, and I have chosen you.* **v 17-** *The poor and needy search for water but there is none; their tongues are parched with thirst. But I the Lord will answer them.*
II Corinthians 2:14- *But thanks be to God, who leads us. . . in Christ and through us spreads everywhere the fragrance of the knowledge of him.*

Friday, July 16, 1999

Isaiah 12:4-5- *Make known among the nations what He has done and proclaim that His name is exalted. Sing to the Lord, for He has done glorious things, let this be known to all the world.*

Another scripture for our message to go around the world! But when? How?!

Friday, August 2, 2002

I recently found this entry in my old journals. My sister, Reba, gave me this scripture back in 1997 for the Center. Haggai 2:7-9 - *I will shake all nations, and the desire of all nations will come, and I will fill this house with glory.* (Could this mean international ministry?) **v 8-** *The silver is mine and the gold is mine.* (Could this be a promise He will provide for us?) **v 9 -** *The glory of this present house will be greater than the glory of the former house and in this place I will grant peace, declares the Lord almighty.*
(Could this signify our expansion?)

I know that the Lord has been pointing out to me scriptures that talk about ministry in other places, like in the islands and "the ends of the earth", and I believe expansion is going to take place. I have enough scriptures that I know we will be going international.

Girls from other countries have taken the training while here in the states. They all say they hope to take CWM to their home countries and open centers. I just don't know if it will happen in my lifetime.

February 25, 2004 - *Today, we officially became an international ministry!*

Today, Ann Chalk, opened the first international center in Sierra Leone, Africa! Here's what happened; When I walked into the office this morning, Sharyl, who works in our office, was preparing something to put into a frame. I assumed she was preparing certificates for the Annual Meeting. I spoke to her and walked past into my office.

In about five minutes, she came in with an e-mail she had framed from Ann. It said, "We are now open and a bona fide Center for Women's Ministries!" In the email, Ann also said, "After years of civil war and women in this county being so traumatized and brutalized in unbelievable and unspeakable ways, God is showing them that He cares for them."

I was so overcome I cried all day. God had given the assurance we would go international, but I never thought it would be in my lifetime. Here I was experiencing growth and expansion that I thought was years in the future. What a gift God gave me that day!!

We now have a presence in 21 countries on five continents. Some of these contacts are emerging centers. Four are locations that are using CWM's Basic Peer Counseling Training (BPCT) in their counseling training programs. Of these, three are Bible Training Schools for pastors. Several countries have women trained in BPCT but have not yet opened Centers.

As we have developed internationally we have had to take a stringent look at our guidelines for operating a CWM. I conferred with the Superintendent of World Missions for the Wesleyan

Church. His advice to me was, "If you are going to be successful world-wide, some guidelines you will have to adapt to each culture. On the basis principles of the ministry you will have to remain firm, but on how you carry out the mission you must be flexible. This is known as a firm center and soft edges." Our BPCT has been deemed 80% applicable to other cultures but 20% must be altered to fit the local society.

These are some challenges we face as we expand:

- Continued translation of our training materials (presently our training is in Spanish, Mandarin Chinese, and Kinyarwandan with other translations in progress)
- Communication is a struggle. Many cultures see no need to keep in communication with headquarters. Internet cafes, for those without computers are expensive, crowded and not easily available. There is corruption in some mail services and postage costs are high.
- Poverty is a problem in many countries.
- Volunteerism is not valued; center director must be paid for credibility and volunteers must be paid for travel and/ or provide lunch.
- Many countries have political unrest, religious terrorism and/or civil war.
- Areas of service deal with poverty, disease, domestic violence, and spousal abuse.

In spite of all these challenges we are rapidly expanding at a rate I would never have expected to happen in my lifetime. What a gift to me and thousands of others. To God be all the glory and praise!

March 3, 2004

Here is another scripture that seems to be a promise of the development of CWM internationally. Genesis 22:18- *All nations on earth will be blessed because you have obeyed me.* Lord, I claim this! I have obeyed you in everything as best I know.

August 1, 2005

Here's a scripture that came to me today. Jeremiah 1:10 *Today I appoint you over nations and kingdoms: to uproot, to tear down, to destroy, to overthrow, to build, to plant.*

"Lord, is this a picture of what we're to do around the world for women?"

To uproot – the mind-set that women are less-than
To tear down – the belief that women are less- than
To destroy – the abuses against women
To overthrow – hopelessness
To plant – hope

Saturday, February 9, 2008

I'm claiming Colossians 1:6 for CWM ministry. *All over the world this gospel is bearing fruit and growing.*

November 3, 2011- *We are in China!*

We received word the Center in Shanghai opened last week! So much has happened over the last 23 years and our expansion has reached 'the world', except I don't know what to do with this level of expansion. It seemed our national spread kind of happened naturally, but this is new and much more complex. Help, Help, Help!

January 1, 2012

Acts 1:8 says, *You will receive power when the Holy Spirit has come upon you,* then talks of the spread of the gospel. This is happening for CWM – Jerusalem, Bloomington; Judea, Indiana; Samaria, The United States, and the ends of the earth, world-wide expansion.

After Jesus command, He left and v. 14 says, *They all joined together constantly in prayer.* It was from this prayer He showed them how to affect the world. "Thank you, Lord! I believe you are telling me through prayer you will show me what to do and how to spread CWM throughout the world. Thank you for this assurance."

The notes in my Leadership Bible says that the *How* of ministry is:

- Received as a vision
- Fulfilled through obedience
- Serves people and advances God
- Brings inward peace
- Vision will last until fulfilled

All of this is something I never thought I would get to see! God has been so good, and we just keep growing and expanding and growing and expanding. We have written our Basic Peer Counselor Training materials that are 14 two-hour sessions. Those are being translated into other languages as we grow. The first translation was Spanish, and the second one was Mandarin Chinese. We will continue to prepare the training for other people that speak different languages.

I can only say this has gone way beyond anything that I ever thought would happen! All I know how to do is to give God the glory and the honor and the praise!

Chapter Fifteen

BACK TO THE FUTURE-INSTRUCTIONS AND DEVELOPMENT OF THE TRAINING VIDEOS

As typically happens in the growth of organizations, seeds are planted, ideas are born, and visions are created long before they come to fruition. It always takes time to plan, the right people to make it happen, and the money to follow through. And then more time and more people and more and more money. Such was the case for a genius part of the ministry that has been vital to existing centers and necessary for emerging centers. In order to move into the future of CWM, the idea needed to be planted way in the past. Reova always tells it best. In her words –

July 5, 1997

I was approached by one of the Center Directors who told me she had been reading in II Kings 4 and felt the story about the widow and the pot of oil had something to do with the finances of the Center. Verse 2 says, *What do you have in your house?. . . Nothing there at all but a little oil.* Verse 7 says, *Go, sell the oil and pay your debts. You and your sons can live on what is left.*

She asked herself, "What does the Center have?" and the answer came back, "A lot of information." She thought, "Maybe we could sell the information?"

This resounded in me – the Training, our support group materials, maybe the history of the CWM? Is it time for us to move ahead marketing these items? "Lord, help me know how to proceed with this, send someone who can organize this."

August 20, 1997

When The Lord gets ready to move, He makes it known. I received confirmation today through Konda, my intercessor, that we are to video the training. (Little did I know we would not get to video this training until 2010 – thirteen years later! It took us a long time to get everything rewritten, professionalized, and the finances procured to make these videos, $40,000. All the rewriting, teaching and editing were donated. We only had to pay for the technical work and duplication. God only knows what it would have cost had we paid for all the teaching and editing.)

This seems like such an unreasonable undertaking. Here's a scripture I felt the Lord gave me for the success of this venture: 2 Corinthians 1:11 *Then many will give thanks on our behalf for the gracious favor granted us in answer to the prayers of many.* "Lord, is this a promise that these videos will be high quality, done with limited stress, and well-received by the public?"

I am confident that these videos will do well, because of the prayers that are being and have been prayed. 2 Corinthians 1:22 says, *He anointed us, set His seal of ownership on us and put His spirit in our hearts. . . guaranteeing what is to come.* The interpretation to me is that 'He has anointed us to do these videos.' Also 2 Corinthians 2:14 says *He uses us to spread the aroma of the knowledge of him everywhere.* Through the center and through the videos the knowledge of Christ spreads everywhere, around the world. This is a powerful promise of our success with the Center and especially these videos. – "We will spread everywhere the knowledge of Christ." And this scripture may not necessarily have anything to do with the videos but seems important. 2 Corinthians 3:2-3- *You yourselves are. . . known and read by everybody. You are the result of our ministry.* I believe this verifies that the healing we see in our clients will be known by the nations (everybody). The healing of many others will be a result of this ministry.

August 1997

We got to work right away organizing the training videos we want to produce. We decided on the following order for the Basic Training, as well as a list to be included called, "Additional Training."

Here's the list we formulated:

1. Introduction – including Confidentiality
2. Communication I – Introduction
3. Communication II – Listening
4. Individual Counseling Techniques
5. Group Facilitating
6. Personal Boundaries
7. Personality Types
8. Healing Process – Introduction
9. Healing Process – Stages
10. Healing Process – Core Issues
11. Codependency
12. Distorted Image of God
13. Personal Accountability

Additional Training Topics:

1. Crisis Situations
2. Divorce

3. Addictions/Compulsions
4. Grief
5. Domestic Violence
6. Shame
7. Anger
8. Sexual Abuse
9. Family Systems
10. Healing the Child Within
11. Depression

I felt a great deal of resistance in preparing to record the videos. It felt like such a big responsibility. However, how can we not do them? My doctorate is in Curriculum Development and Supervision and with the years I spent in the classroom doing exactly that, the human preparation was certainly in place.

Here's some scriptures that seemed like promises that the videos should be high quality, done with limited stress, and be well received by the public:

2 Corinthians 1:11- *Then many will give thanks on our behalf for the gracious favor granted us in answer to the prayers of many.*

2 Corinthians 1:22- *He anointed us, set His seal of ownership on us and put His spirit in our hearts. . . guaranteeing what is to come.*

To *put His spirit in our hearts* meant to me that He is able to talk to us and show us what we should do, and we will be obedient. *Guaranteeing what is to come* meant to me that we will be successful with this venture.

2 Corinthians 2:14- *But thanks be to God who always leads us in triumphal procession in Christ.* We will triumph through this venture with Christ. *Through us spreads everywhere the fragrance of the knowledge of Him.* This is a powerful promise of our success. We will spread everywhere the knowledge of Christ."

2 Corinthians 3:5-6 - *Not that we are competent in ourselves to claim anything for ourselves, but our competency comes from God. He has made us competent.*

My fear that these videos will not be done well has been very great. My concern is that I am not enough of a perfectionist to do them well. I have had to go back before the Lord repeatedly praying that my fear will be taken away. He continues to give me wonderful promises that we will be successful.

January 10, 2000

We need the money to do these training videos. I reminded the Lord He had promised, if I would be obedient, He would provide the people, materials, know-how and money to get these done. I'm trusting Him to do this.

It's rather surprising that this is such an issue for me. Normally I would have jumped at the chance to make these. Maybe God is stripping away pride. It's probably true that I couldn't do this until God had stripped away all the self- sufficiency and made me totally dependent upon Him.

I talked to my college friend, who, after reading about the videos in the monthly intercessor newsletter said, "Reova, get rid of the 'if' – you have to do the videos. You should have done them two years ago!" What a pointed reprimand!

March, 2003

We held our first Leadership Intensive Training (LIT) this week. This week of exhaustive training was designed because we realized, as the ministry developed, we could not personally train, with so small a headquarters' staff, all those from other states and countries who were interested in taking the Basic Peer Counseling Training (BPCT).

Twelve women from eight states and two foreign countries comprised our initial LIT. We had spent months and months designing the week to accomplish the following:

- Teach the BPCT (14 two-hour sessions)
- Train the potential leaders in the Center Director and Procedures manuals
- Expose them to devotions designed to deepen their personal relationship with God
- Provide processing time to deal with unhealed areas in their individual lives

We began each morning with devotions. I spoke on Prayer, Obedience, Faith, Hope, and Love, each one on a different morning. The intent was to portray how all five of these work together in the Christian life. Response from the participants was that these times of being exposed to God's Word were the highlights of their day. "Thank you Jesus, your Word is powerful!"

June 21, 2009

Tomorrow a crew from Indianapolis is coming to tape my story. "Lord, you know how I dread this and seldom feel satisfied with the outcome." As I was laboring over this the Lord impressed upon me to fast. I've been preparing training for our leadership retreat on fasting. One of the times to fast is when we are required to do a difficult task. I resolved not to eat tomorrow until the taping is finished.

I have lived this, recorded it all in journals, and told it many, many times. "I'm asking you, Lord, to take over and simply empower this taping in a way that brings glory and honor to you. Help me to say the things you want said and leave out those you don't want shared. If this is successful, it won't be me, it will simply be you."

Acts 2:11- *We hear them declaring the wonders of God.* This is what I want for the taping- that anyone who hears or sees the video will hear me declare the wonders of God.

June 22, 2009

"Lord, I want these words to be your words." I'm still trying to decide whether to include the offer from Indiana Wesleyan University when I tell my story in the video. I think including it shows a couple of things: One, how Satan tried to sidetrack me from God's best for me, and two, that there has to be a sacrifice of the thing we hold most dear if we want God's best.

We started taping and it simply flowed out of me for 36 minutes, absolutely filled with emotion. It was very evident the Holy Spirit was directing the whole thing. When I finished the camera crew said, "Amen, that was wonderful." They felt they had what they needed, and we did not need to do any re-taping. WOW! They told me the message was very powerful. When I reviewed the tape, I was so filled with emotion. The message of God's faithfulness seemed so powerful. They said very little editing would be necessary. "Lord, I was obedient. I fasted and you came through. Thank you, you are faithful. It turned out better than I could have asked for! I'm asking you, Lord, to send this taping around the world to tell what you will do in response to obedience and faith. I can't express how pleased I am with the results. You are so gracious, good and kind. I want the world to know you are faithful. Praise Your name!"

Fall, 2010

We were finally able to tape both BPCT trainings and the devotionals that I did each morning at LIT this year! The production went well. Every teacher led her session professionally and the production company was excellent and easy to work with. It really was a fun experience for all of us, once we got past the initial nerves. I am so relieved and grateful to God!

Another thing I am really thanking God for is the situation with copyrights for these training materials. It appears we are safe within the copyright guidelines and for the most part only need to give credit. I plan to write for a few more permissions after we assess what percentage of their materials were used directly. We also need to inform how we plan to market our materials and see if that makes a difference in some prior permissions we have received. I also plan to prepare a letter to our lawyer, for confirmation on the responses we get. "Lord, walk before me on this." I've been troubled off and on, worried, and lost sleep over this copyright stuff for years. We have a contact from Nigeria who was the Director of the country's medical library, and she helped us confirm some of the government guidelines I read. This also agreed with confirmation from the research librarian at the Monroe County Library. This was a big relief yesterday. "Help me, Lord, to construct these letters and please give us favor. Thank you, Lord."

October, 2010

I got three letters written today about the copyright for training materials. That has been such struggle for me! "Lord, go before us and give us favor." I also asked for an appointment with one of our contributing authors, hoping to get an endorsement from him. "Lord, guide all this also! I am so relieved at this point over the copyright issue. I am depending on you that we haven't gone astray."

December, 2010

We have been granted permission to use the contributing authors' materials in our BPCT curriculum! "Thank you, Lord!"

Prayer   *Love*

OBEDIENCE
Faith   Hope

Love – The Most powerful force in life. If we are having trouble trusting God we simply do not understand how much He loves us.

Prayer – The Most Powerful channel of Communication. The world is helpless against our prayers.

Obedience – The most rewarding action. Obedience is always our choice, but if we struggle with obedience, something else is in competition for our love.

Faith – The Greatest asset. As faith grows, it moves through trials of understanding God's character and, like Job, is finally able to say, "Though He slay me, yet will I trust Him."

Hope – The worst thing to be without. Hope begins when the memory of what is lost is replaced with a longing for what can take its place. Hope is always life-giving.

Faith, Hope, and Love are inner transformations. Prayer and Obedience are the outward manifestations that bring about these inner transformations.

-REOVA MEREDITH

Chapter Sixteen

HIS GOODNESS GOES ON AND ON AND ON

God's plan for CWM had been unfolding now for decades and its boundaries were ever expanding. His plan, however, wasn't just about growth and expansion. As He is an expert in everything, He was, of course, proving Himself to be a great business executive. He was making sure the ministry grew deep, as well as wide. Not only did the trainings need to be spiritually, educationally, and clinically sound, the health of the organization also needed to operate like any excellent business. God kept His promise and continued to provide the people, the know-how, and the resources to accomplish His plan. Reova's final journal entries tell it best…

Fall, 2011

From a family foundation, we were given finances to underwrite salary for an assistant for the Executive Director to take over some of my responsibilities. I talked to JoAnne Rodes, Center director at DuBois County center in Indiana. She told me she and her daughter-in-law had an interesting conversation within the last month. Her daughter asked her, "Mom, if you could have your dream job, what would it be?" JoAnne's reply was "I would love to work at CWM headquarters." God works in His amazing mysterious ways.

The details have not been worked out but it appears I will have someone to help with my responsibilities. Praise the Lord!

December 22, 2011

I'm thinking about JoAnne coming to H.Q. and giving her leadership over the existing centers and development in the U.S. But, I feel like I'm giving up the area of the ministry that I know about. Facing the international development and the whole marketing scheme feels overwhelming – I simply don't know what to do. It's kind of like it was 22 years ago – just moving into uncharted territory. "Lord, I desperately need your guidance and direction. Help me to seek you with every decision."

Maybe this is my directive: This from Madame Guyon: "The only work you are required now to do is to give your most intense attention to His still small voice within."

January 1, 2012

JoAnne joined the staff at headquarters!

2011 - 2012

Konda and I spent all of 2011 and part of 2012 editing the training videos and the devotionals. Konda is a lot better at this than I am. I struggled but she did wonderfully. We had to edit each video three times, sending them back to the video company each time for more revision.

August 12, 2012

One of our donors had told me months ago to not 'cheat' in what we needed to do to make this DVD training package what we wanted it to be. We were to let them know if we needed more money. We needed $5740 to pay for the marketing expenses. Their initial generous donation of $40,000 paid for the taping and editing of the training and the devotional but did not cover the marketing expenses of packaging, a promo video, display unit and rack cards. We received another check for $6000 to cover additional expenses. Praise the Lord!

August 24, 2012

These training videos have been a three-year project. It has taken over two years to edit and revise the training. It is nearly finished. What will I be doing when it is finished – writing the history?

June 27-28, 2014 -25th Anniversary of CWM!

We decided to have the 25th anniversary celebration in June instead of October, because when we first opened our doors in 1989 the approval for our 501c3 came in June. Also, we were to have Leadership Intensive Training during November of the same year, and with our small office staff it would be almost impossible to prepare for both in the fall.

The celebration for our 25th was scheduled as a two-day event. Friday, the 27th, the Bloomington Center had an open house for the community from 3:00 to 6:00 pm. (It is really their 25th since they were the initial center.) Their volunteers showed up and a couple of significant people from the community – a local Judge and a former Bloomington Mayor. We were pleased and surprised the former mayor came as she shared she had been badly hurt by the 'church' when she was young and remained angry at the religious community.

I spent time talking to the Judge who had been my boys Little League Coach about 40 years earlier.

He talked about hearing and knowing God's voice when He speaks. He uses *My Utmost for His Highest by Oswald Chambers* for devotions in the morning.

The Bloomington conference room was beautifully decorated with yellow and silver. The volunteers served punch, coffee, and cookies. Serving birthday cake was reserved for Saturday as part of the anniversary celebration.

Forty-five members attended the annual meeting. Volunteers from North Carolina, Georgia, Kentucky, and Missouri were present as well as volunteers from Indiana (5 states). All of our present Board of Directors were able to attend.

The meeting agenda consisted of all the typical ministry reports and I gave a State of the Ministry address. We also gave out our Friend of the Ministry Awards, which it seems everyone enjoys and looks forward to. In addition, we had sharing by our Center Directors and a beautiful song that one of our Owen County volunteers accompanied with sign language and a testimony. All of these elements came together as a perfect example of what we do and how our clients find healing and wholeness.

While this celebration was happening on Friday, our headquarters' office staff was preparing for the celebration on Saturday. Out in the Warehouse we set up displays of memorabilia from our 'opening' days, displays of picture albums from the various centers. We laid out the first training manual which was about a half-inch thick, then the four- inch binder which is the training manual of today and the 2 ½ inch binder that is the student book. We also showed the training video and the DVD of me giving the early history on a loop for continuous play.

The booth display, that we use for conferences, was set up with the introduction DVD of the Basic Peer Counseling Training playing on a loop. That booth is so impressive! It looks very professional. What a gift to us!

A table with cards and souvenir pens was prepared for participants to write what Center for Women's Ministries has meant to them.

Reading those cards was wonderful reminders of why we do what we do.

Ann Dillon had sorted out and brought boxes and boxes of books, tape sets, DVDs, CDs and set up a give-away table. She had only two boxes left when the celebration was over. Her tables of 'gifts' were a real attraction.

There was a table with bottles of water iced in a small tub. This was very important since only the offices in the Warehouse are air conditioned. Staff has been praying for months that it would not be too hot for people to be comfortable. The daily temperatures had been reaching the high 80's each afternoon prior to our celebration. The Warehouse commercial fans had been stolen so the building was very warm during the day. One of our friends and supporters brought huge fans from his business and set them around in our space on Friday evening, and another came in about midnight to open the doors and allow the fans to draw in the evening air. It was amazing how cool the building was. No one seemed to complain about being too hot. In fact, the reports were that people were very comfortable. Thank you Lord, for that wonderful answer to prayer.

At 2:30 we met back in the Warehouse for the 25th Anniversary Celebration where 65 people had gathered. After the welcome we enjoyed worshipful music and a historical video of the last 25 years that included pictures of all the centers, years they opened, and all the center directors. A particular highlight accompanying the video was our first landlord who played his harmonica and sang, "Jesus Made a Believer Out of Me". What a blessing and testament to God's faithfulness and transforming power! The meeting concluded with the sharing of our 10- year goals and the future social media development.

Later that evening, sixty-eight people gathered at the Cornerstone Community Church for a lovely dinner where I was beautifully honored for being the founder and executive director.

I was so happy to have my family come for the occasion, including my brother and my sister, Rita. The focus of the entire night was about being obedient to the call of God and the results of obedience. I got to introduce my family, the Board of Directors, and the Headquarters Staff. The office staff presented me with an afghan personalized with "Center for Women's Ministries" and our scriptural directive of Isaiah 61: 1-3. We enjoyed more music and a highlights video of people involved in the ministry over the last 25 years. These were all made into a memory book and presented to me by the Bloomington Center volunteers. What a beautiful evening!!! We had prayed for months that God would get all the glory, honor and praise for all we did that weekend. I believe He was pleased!! So many of our ladies' husbands and sons helped us in ways that demanded more expertise and strength than we had. They were all so instrumental in making the 25th Anniversary celebration a success. Several of them said, "I never realized how extensive or involved the Center for Ministries was. Now I have a new appreciation for what my wife does and how important it is."

Not long after celebrating 25 years as a ministry, God continued to move the ministry toward excellence by providing the people, the resources, and the know-how for an extensive rebranding endeavor and social media campaign. The next few years would involve quite a learning curve for everyone in the ministry. Growth always brings challenges, and the Center Directors and volunteers have risen to meet those challenges in gracious and Christlike ways.

In addition to the rebranding and social media changes, the Board of Directors of CWM also pursued developing a Strategic plan initiative for both short-term and long-term goals. As this began just as Covid hit the nation, the workload for this great task became increasingly convoluted, even with the introduction of online meeting capabilities. Still, the board and HQ staff worked tirelessly to produce a Strategic Plan that will help steer the ministry into the future and whatever it may hold.

In the midst of all this, more international development emerged. This was an interesting result of a seminary student from India visiting the CWM booth at the American Association of Christian Counselors international convention. He was studying in the U. S. at a seminary in St. Louis, Missouri, and was compelled to take CWM back to the women in India. Here is Reova's last journal entry....

Spring, 2016

We arranged to hold a special training at the seminary where several students from Rwanda and Kenya in Africa and southern India registered for the classes. They each have a deep concern for the people in their countries. Common occurrence of polygamy and infidelity resulting from the shame of infertility, more of the horrors and trauma of genocide, dilemmas of cultures that reinforce shame and a 'less-than' mentality and so much more. The question they asked more than any other is "What can we do?" It can be a helpless feeling until we remember what their people need most is Jesus.

Following several weeks of Saturday trainings, the graduation ceremony was held on Saturday, May 7, 2016. It was a precious and emotional time for everyone involved. One of the graduates from India called this day unforgettable. He remarked that he was unable to speak for some time following the foot-washing part of the ceremony. He was shocked at the humbling impact it had on him, as he had never before experienced anything like that.

All of the students expressed overwhelming appreciation for the training, the kindness and concern of the trainers, and for the opportunity to take new hope back to the women of their countries.

I am overwhelmed at getting to see God's plan for taking this ministry throughout the world, as I believe He told me He would do. I don't know any more about how He will accomplish this than I did in the early days. But I know His faithfulness. I'm thinking about a quote I read years ago. The author said that once God purifies our motives and our faith has been tested, He will release His abundance in the measure He can trust us to be used for His glory. I pray I have been found trustworthy for Him to use, for He sure is releasing His abundance.

Tonight, as I, Paula, write the closing paragraphs of God's amazing story of The Center for Women's Ministries that I have had the honor to share with you, I am sitting on a plane somewhere over the Middle East headed back to India. As I, and others, have prayed so many prayers over this writing project, it is not lost on me that as I finish writing, God has me headed to the uttermost parts of the world – to one of the very places Reova's final journal entry reaches. I didn't plan it this way, only God could do that.

How humbling for all of us who have been a part of CWM to know that God used each of us in our own small way to be one of the people "He promised He would provide" in taking His healing to women all around the world one Center at a time! Reova was obedient and God fulfilled His promise to her at every turn. There is no end to the healing God desires to extend to women everywhere. There is no end to the promises He longs to fulfill through each of us in centers here in the United States and all around the world. He only asks one thing from each of us… Obedience.

Reova had learned the interconnectedness of these beautiful concepts God was showing her. Through prayer, she learned how faith, hope, love are interconnected. Hope is built on love and hope expands as love grows. Faith is also built as love grows. And while, as I Corinthians 13 says, *The greatest is of these is love,* none are reachable without prayer, faith, and hope, and none are learned without obedience.

Printed in the United States
by Baker & Taylor Publisher Services